# The Best In COUNTRY LOVE SONGS

Project Manager: Carol Cuellar
Art Director: Frank Milone
Cover Photography: Roberto Santos

# CONTENTS

# ME AND YOU

Words and Music by
SKIP EWING and RAY HERNDON

Slowly ♩ = 72

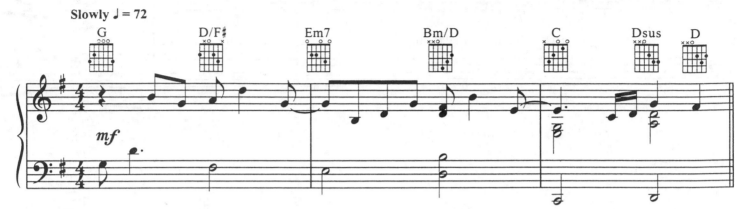

Verse:

1. Or-di-nar-y? No,___ real-ly don't think so,___ not a love this true.___

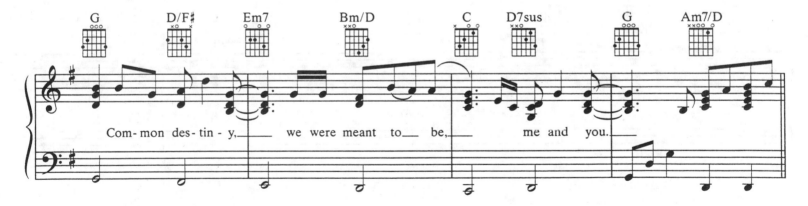

Com-mon des-tin-y,___ we were meant to___ be,___ me and you.___

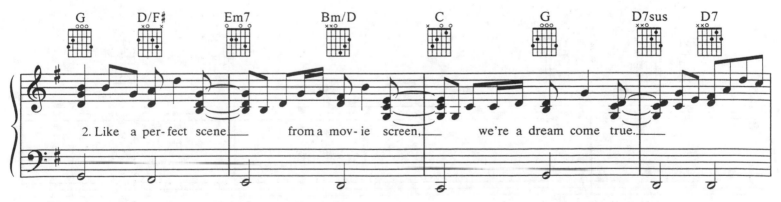

2. Like a per-fect scene___ from a mov-ie screen,___ we're a dream come true.

Me and You - 3 - 1

4

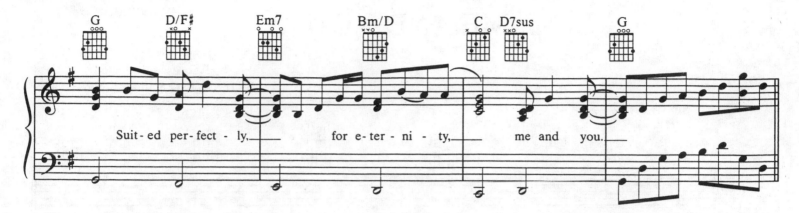

Suit-ed per-fect-ly,\_\_\_ for e-ter-ni-ty,\_\_\_ me and you.\_\_\_

𝄋 *Chorus:*

Ev-ery-day\_\_ I need\_\_ you e-ven more,\_\_\_\_\_ and\_ the night-time too.

There's\_no way\_\_\_ I could ev-er let\_\_ you go\_\_

e-ven if I want-ed to.

*Verse:*

3. Ev - ery - day I live,___ try my best to give___ all I have to you.
4. *(Inst. solo ad lib....*
5. *See additional lyrics*

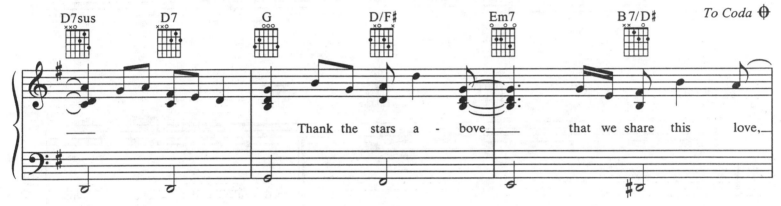

*To Coda*

Thank the stars a - bove___ that we share this love,

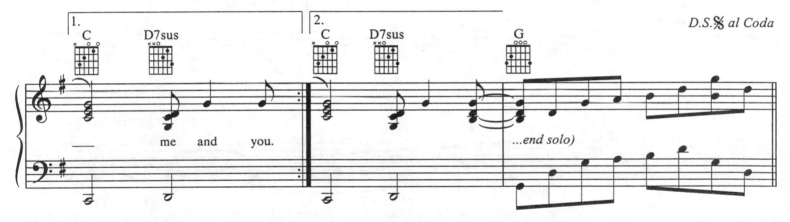

*D.S. al Coda*

1. ___ me and you.

2. ...end solo)

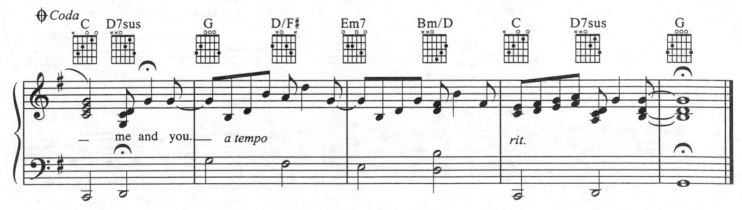

*Coda*

___ me and you. *a tempo* *rit.*

*Verse 5:*
Ordinary?
No, really don't think so.
Just a precious few
Ever make it last,
Get as lucky as
Me and you.

# I CAN LOVE YOU LIKE THAT

Words and Music by
STEVE DIAMOND, MARIBETH DERRY
and JENNIFER KIMBALL

Ju - li - et._____ All this time that you've been wait - ing,_____
it comes to___ you. You dream of love that's ev - er - last - ing,_____ well

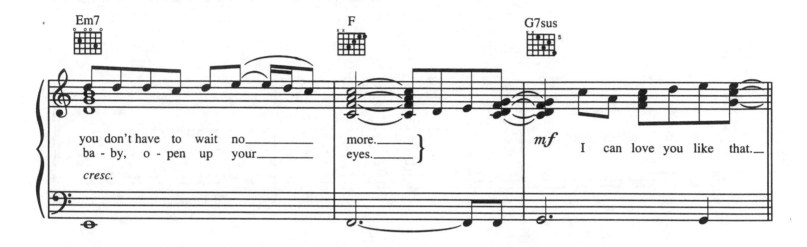

you don't have to wait no_____ more._____
ba - by, o - pen up your_____ eyes._____

*cresc.*

*mf* I can love you like that.___

*Chorus:*

___ I would make you my world,___ move heav - en and earth___ if you were my girl.___

___ I will give you my heart,___ be all that you need,___ show you you're ev -

-'ry-thing that's pre-cious to me. If you give me a chance,

I can love you like that. 2. I

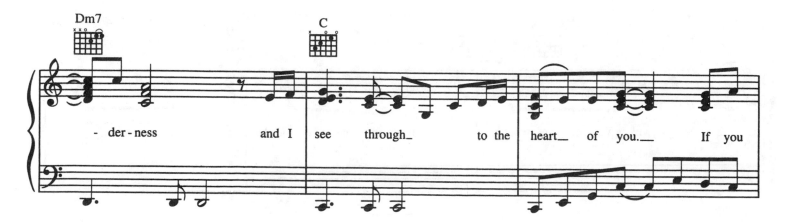

_____ You want ten-der-ness, I've got ten-

-der-ness and I see through_ to the heart_ of you._ If you

*From the Warner Bros. Film "PURE COUNTRY"*

# I CROSS MY HEART

Words and Music by
STEVE DORFF and ERIC KAZ

I Cross My Heart - 4 - 1

From here_ on af - ter,___ let's stay the way we are_ right now,___ and share

all the love_ and laugh-ter___ that a life-time will al low.

*cresc.*

**Chorus:**

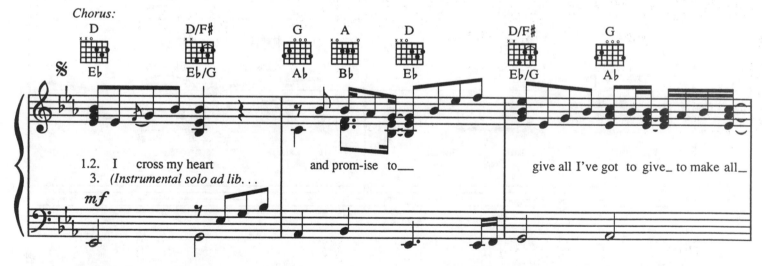

1.2. I cross my heart and prom-ise to__ give all I've got to give_ to make all_

3. *(Instrumental solo ad lib. . .*

*mf*

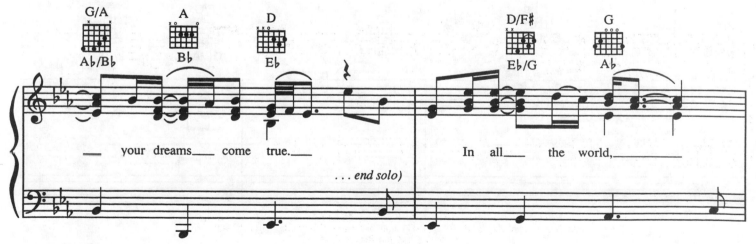

_ your dreams___ come true.___ In all___ the world,_____

*. . . end solo)*

12

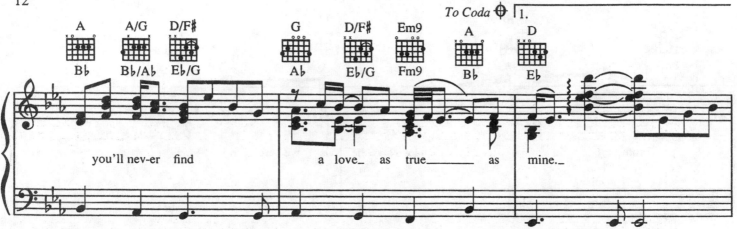

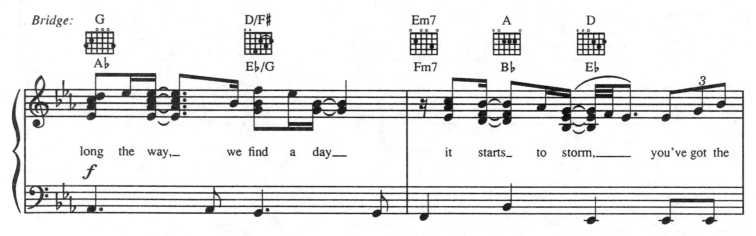

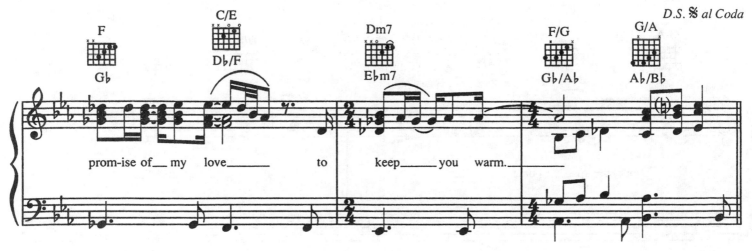

I Cross My Heart - 4 - 3

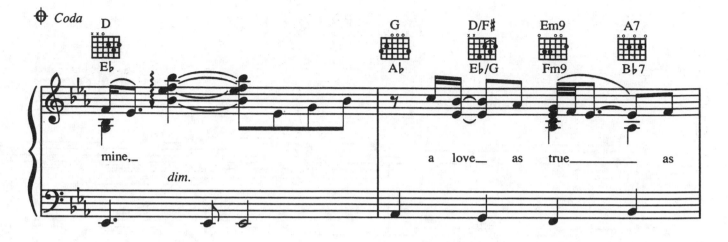

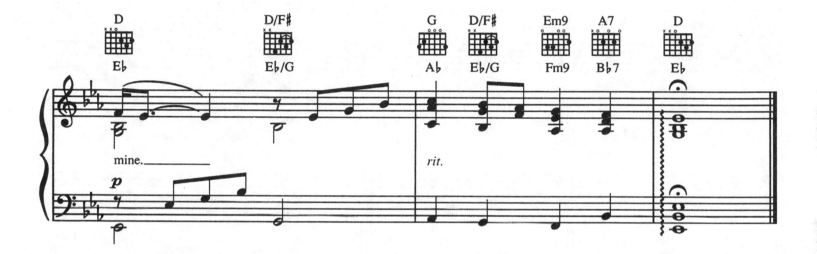

*Verse 2:*
You will always be the miracle
That makes my life complete;
And as long as there's a breath in me,
I'll make yours just as sweet.
As we look into the future,
It's as far as we can see,
So let's make each tomorrow
Be the best that it can be.
*(To Chorus:)*

# ALL I HAVE

Words and Music by
BETH NIELSEN CHAPMAN
and ERIC KAZ

All I have\_\_\_ is all\_\_\_ I need,\_\_\_ and it all\_\_\_

\_ comes down\_\_\_ to you\_\_\_\_\_ and me.\_\_\_ How\_ far\_\_\_

\_ a - way\_\_\_ this world\_\_\_ be - comes\_\_\_ in the har -

# ANGELS AMONG US

Words and Music by
BECKY HOBBS and DON GOODMAN

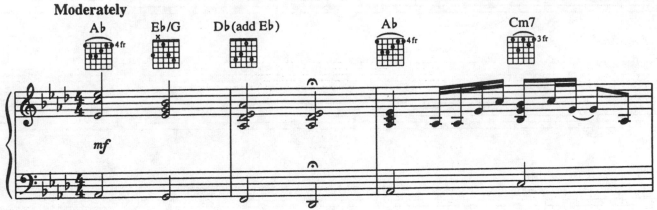

Spoken: I was walking home from school
(See additional lyrics)

on a cold winter day,

took a short cut through the woods and I lost my way. It was getting late

and I was scared and alone, then a kind old man took my hand and led me home.

Angels among Us - 4 - 1

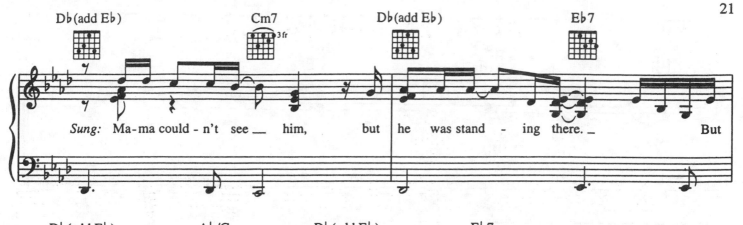

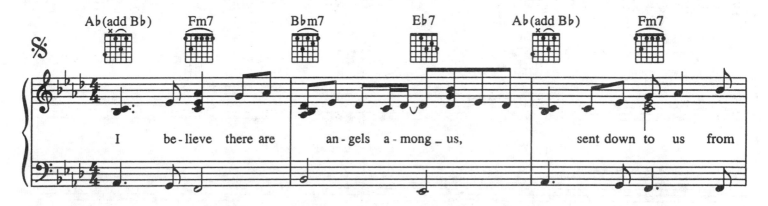

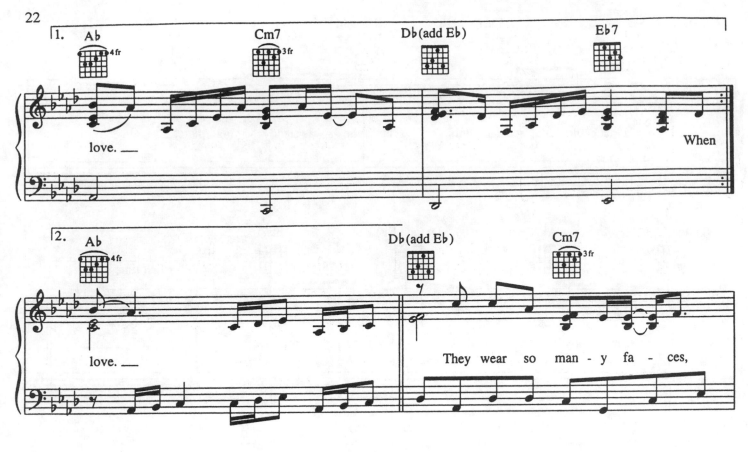

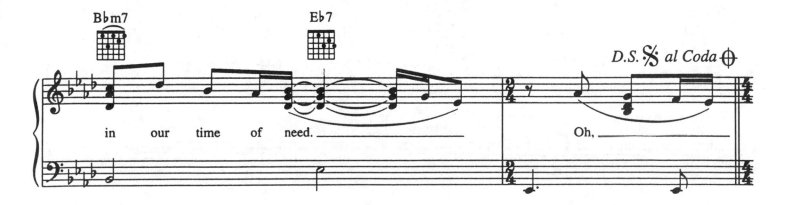

*Repeat and fade*

I be - lieve there are an - gels a - mong us

*a tempo*

sent down to us from some - where up a - bove. They come to you and me ___ in

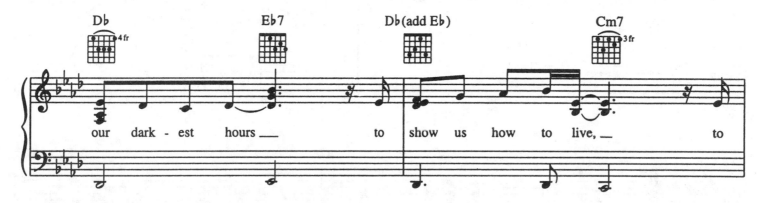

our dark - est hours ___ to show us how to live, ___ to

teach us how to give ___ to guide us with a light of ___ love. ___

**Additional lyrics**

When life held troubled times and had me down on my knees,
There's always been someone to come along and comfort me.
A kind word from a stranger, to lend a helping hand,
A phone call from a friend just to say I understand.
Now, ain't it kind of funny, at the dark end of the road,
Someone lights the way with just a single ray of hope.

*(To Chorus)*

Angels among Us - 4 - 4

# ANOTHER WORLD

By JOHN LEFFLER
and RALPH SCHUCKETT

Moderate rock ♩ = 120

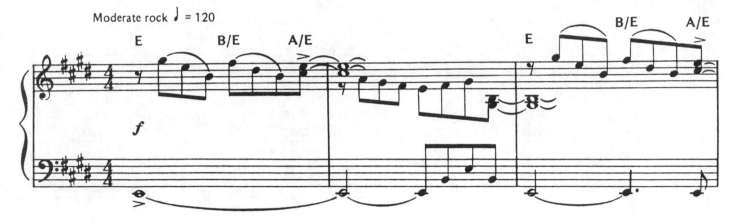

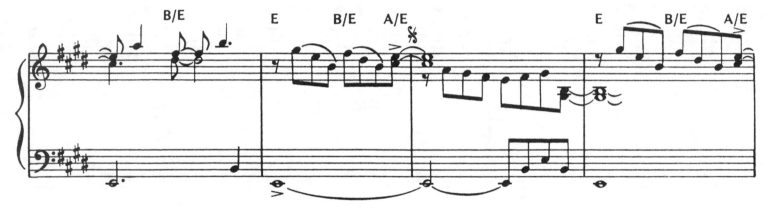

I've al-ways seen my-self ___ as a reck-less gam - bler,

risk-ing all that I had, ___ when-ev - er I could.

Another World - 3 - 1

Another World - 3 - 2

*Verse 2:*
All my life I've been called a hopeless romantic,
Waiting for my prince to take me away.
But when I found you I felt different,
Than I've ever felt before.
Suddenly I was taking no chances
By walking through your door.
You are my . . .
*(To Chorus:)*

# FOREVER'S AS FAR AS I'LL GO

Words and Music by
MIKE REID

Forever's As Far As I'll Go - 3 - 1

It's best that you know___ where you stand___ with me._____

cresc.

I will

mf

*Chorus:*

give you___ my heart_____ ___ faith - ful___ and true,___ and all the love it can hold_____

that's all I can do.___ But I've thought a - bout_____ how long I'll___ love you,

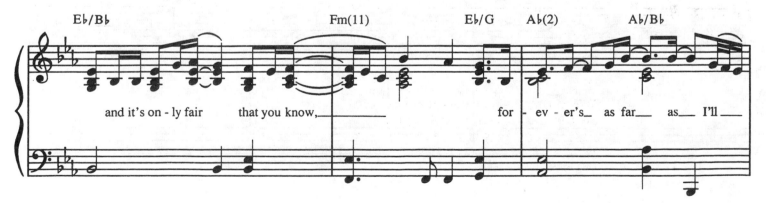

and it's on - ly fair that you know,_____ for - ev - er's___ as far___ as___ I'll___

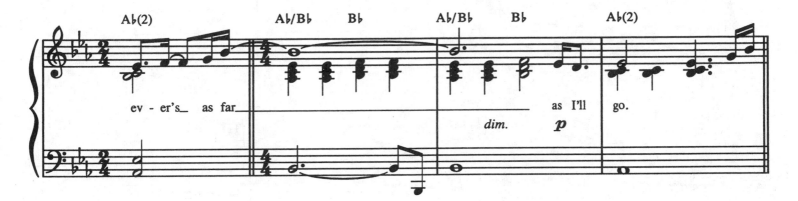

*Verse 2:*
When there's age around my eyes and gray in your hair,
And it only takes a touch to recall the love we've shared.
I won't take for granted that you know my love is true.
Each night in your arms, I will whisper to you...
*(To Chorus:)*

Forever's As Far As I'll Go - 3 - 3

# THE CLOSER YOU GET

Words and Music by
MARK GRAY and
JAMES P. PENNINGTON

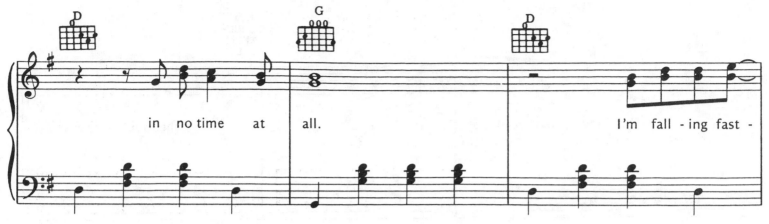

in no time at all. I'm fall -ing fast -

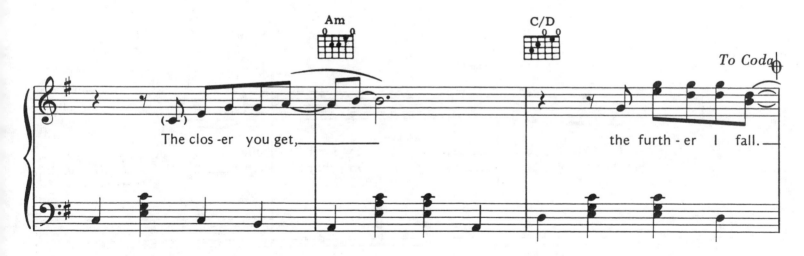

er and fast - er and fast - er with no time to stall.

The clos -er you get, the furth - er I fall.

The clos - er you get

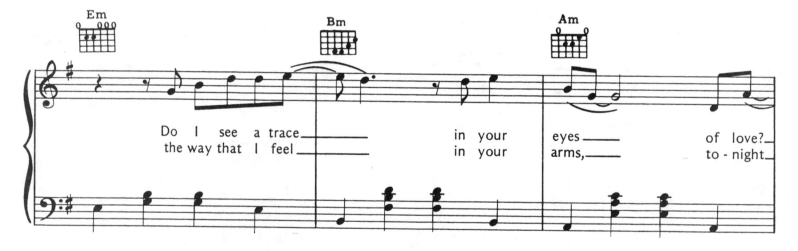

The Closer You Get - 4 - 3

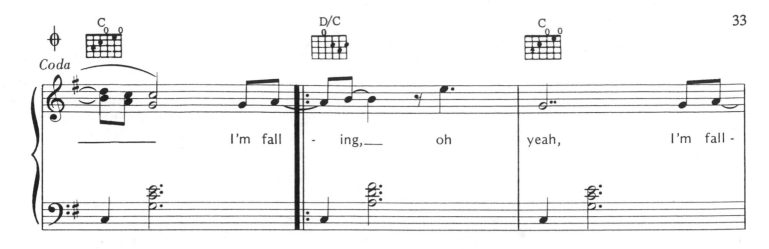

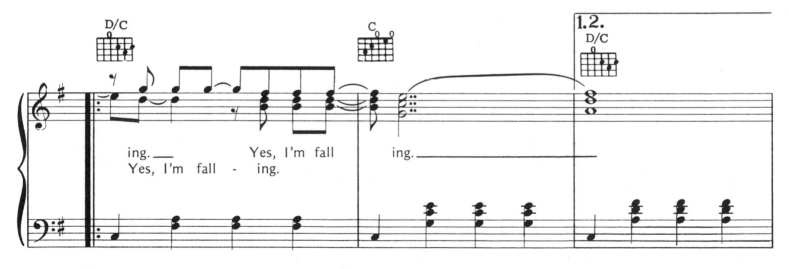

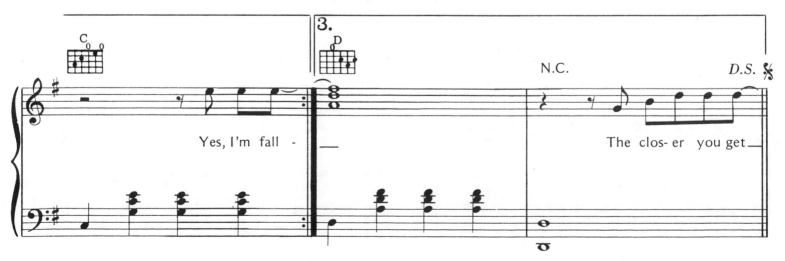

The Closer You Get - 4 - 4

# FALL IN LOVE

Words and Music by
KENNY CHESNEY, BUDDY BROCK
and KIM WILLIAMS

Moderately fast ♩ = 136

1. A lit-tle

Verse:

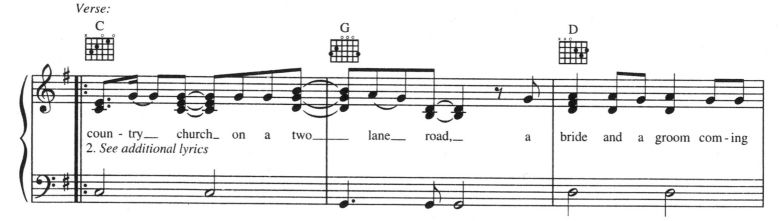

coun-try__ church__ on a two__ lane__ road,__ a bride and a groom com-ing
2. See additional lyrics

out the door._____ White__ lace dress and a red bou-quet, "Just__

Fall in Love - 4 - 1

_Married" writ-ten on a blue Chev-ro-let._____ Don't\_

_Chorus:_

\_\_ that make you wan-na fall in\_\_ love?\_ Don't\_\_\_\_ that look like a

pic-ture of us?\_\_ A match\_\_ made in heav-en if there ev-er\_\_ was,\_ don't\_

\_\_ that make you wan-na fall?_____ That\_\_ just makes me wan-na

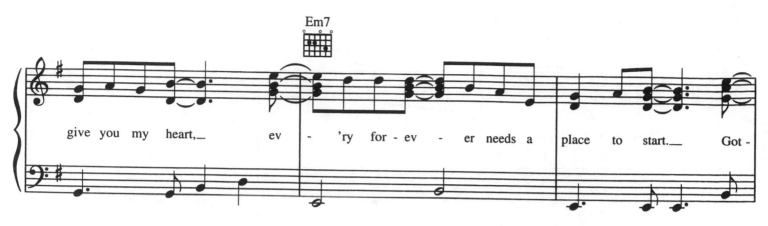

give you my heart,\_\_ ev - 'ry for - ev - er needs a place to start.\_\_ Got -

- ta be a sign from\_\_ up a - bove.\_\_ Don't_____ that make you wan - na

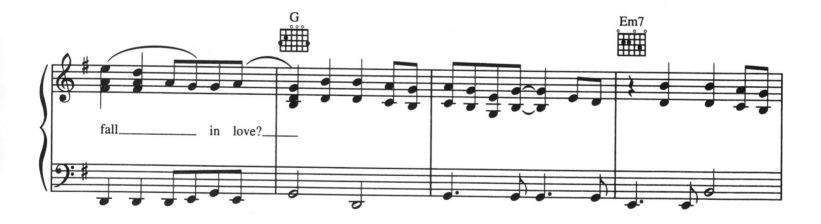

fall_____ in love?\_\_\_\_\_

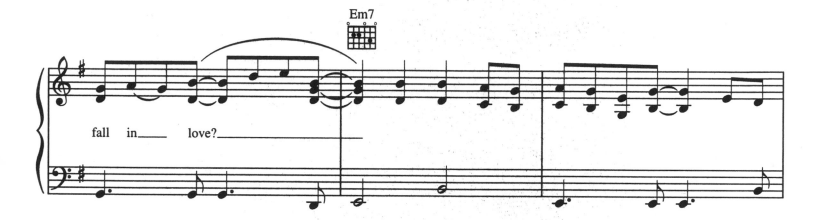

*Verse 2:*
Old folks sitting in a front porch swing
Still holding hands like they were sixteen.
Fifty good years, they're a lover's dream.
Darling, that could be you and me.
*(To Chorus:)*

# I DO

Words and Music by
PAUL BRANDT

I Do - 4 - 1

40

And did I say\_\_ my love\_\_\_\_\_ is true?\_\_\_\_ *dim.* Ba-by, I

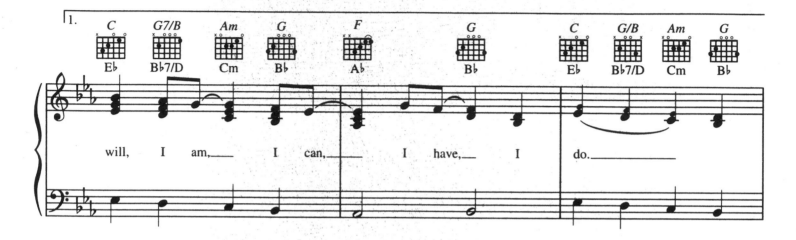

will, I am,\_\_ I can,\_\_ I have,\_ I do.\_\_\_\_

will, I am,\_\_ I can,\_\_ I have,\_ I do.\_ *mp*

*mf* (Instrumental solo...

I Do - 4 - 3

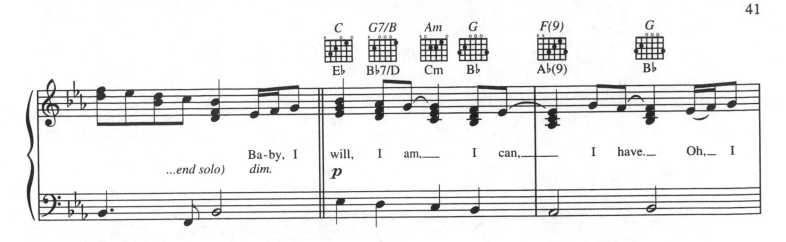

*Verse 3:*
I know the time will disappear,
But this love we're building on will always be here.
No way that this is sinking sand,
On this solid rock we'll stand forever...
*(To Chorus:)*

# I LOVE THE WAY YOU LOVE ME

Words and Music by
VICTORIA SHAW and
CHUCK CANNON

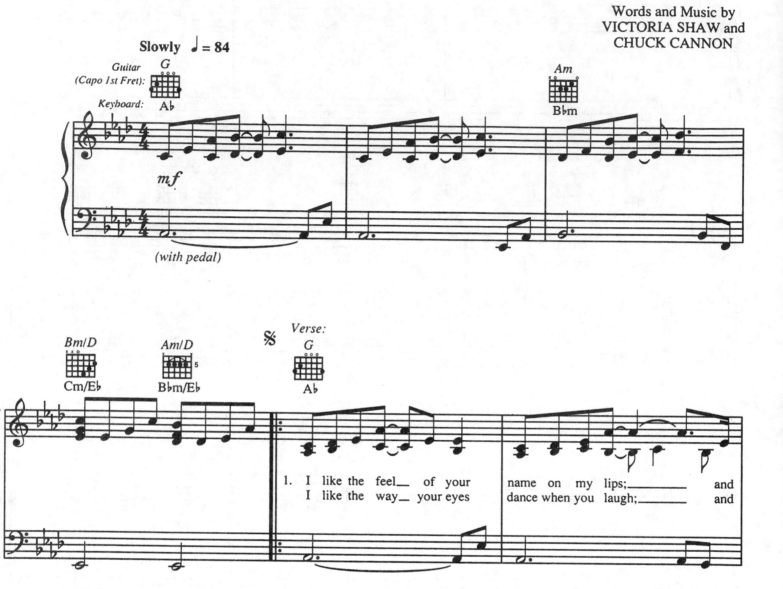

1. I like the feel___ of your name on my lips;_____ and
I like the way___ your eyes dance when you laugh;_____ and

I like the sound___ of your sweet,___ gen - tle___ kiss;___ the way that your fin - gers___ run___
how you en - joy___ your two hour___ bath;_ and how you con - vinced___ me to dance___

I Love the Way You Love Me - 4 - 1

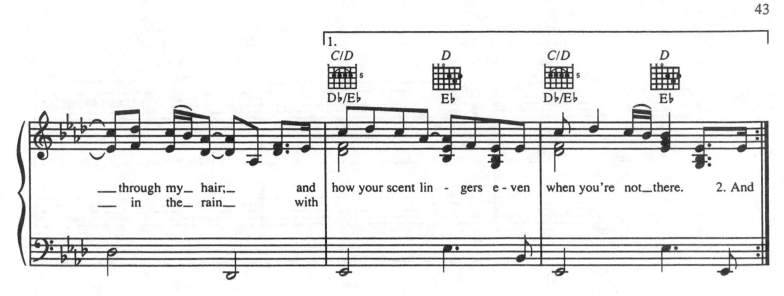

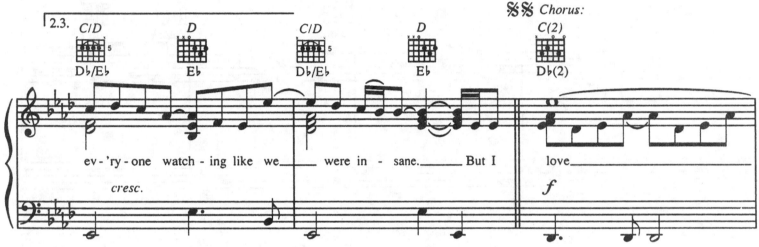

44

so com-plete-ly. I___ love_____ the way____ you love____

*To Coda* ⊕  |1.                                                                                      *D.S.* %

___ me.

|2.                                                                *Bridge:*

And I could list___ a mil - lion things___

I love to like a - bout___ you,                 but they all come_ down to___

D.S.S. 𝄋 𝄋 al Coda

one___ rea - son, I could nev - er live___ with-out___ you. I

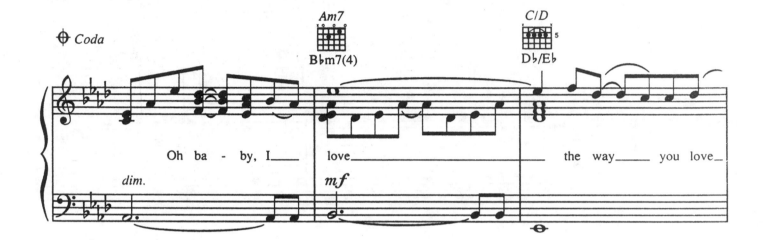

Oh ba - by, I___ love_____ the way___ you love___

___ me._____ dim. e rit.

Verse 3:
I like to imitate ol' Jerry Lee
While you roll your eyes when I'm slightly off key.
And I like the innocent way that you cry
At sappy, old movies you've seen hundreds of times.
(To Chorus:)

I Love the Way You Love Me - 4 - 4

# I NEVER KNEW LOVE

Words and Music by
WILL ROBINSON and LARRY BOONE

I Never Knew Love - 4 - 1

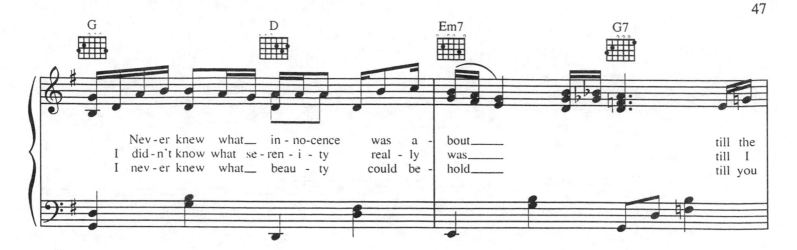

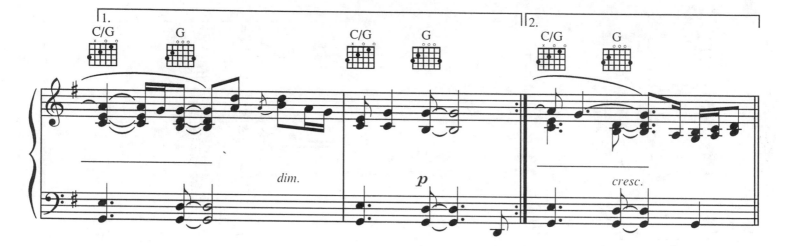

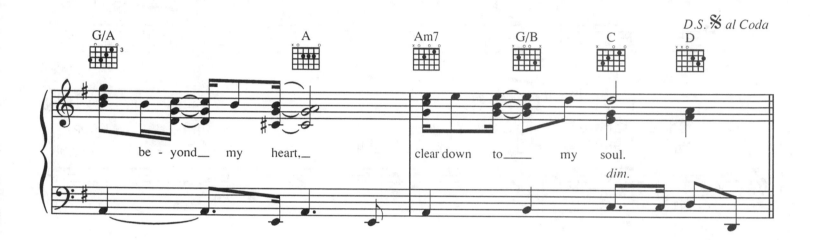

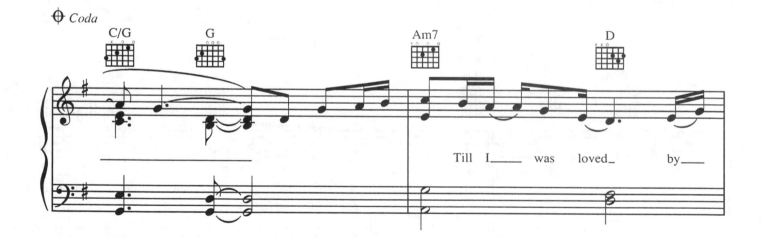

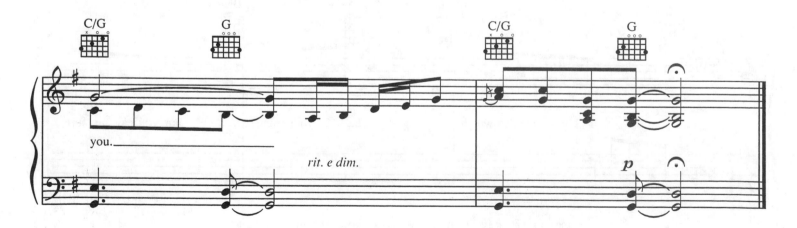

I Never Knew Love - 4 - 4

# I SWEAR

Words and Music by
GARY BAKER and FRANK MYERS

I Swear - 4 - 1

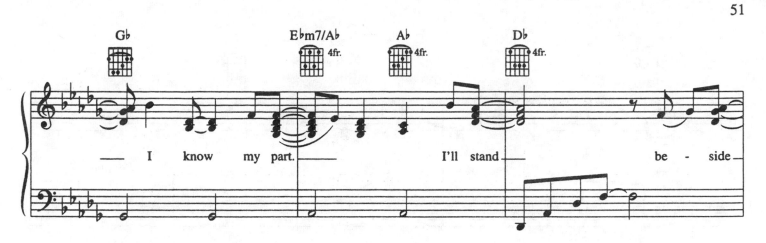

I know my part. I'll stand be- side

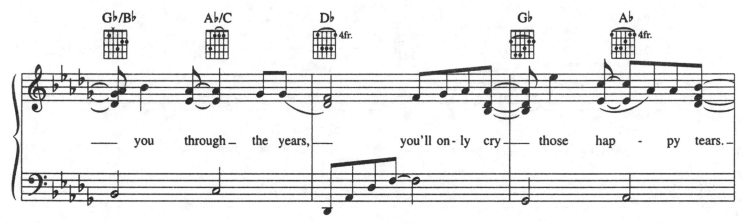

you through the years, you'll on- ly cry those hap - py tears.

And though I'll make mis- takes, I'll nev- er break your heart.

I swear, by the moon and the stars in the sky,

I Swear - 4 - 2

52

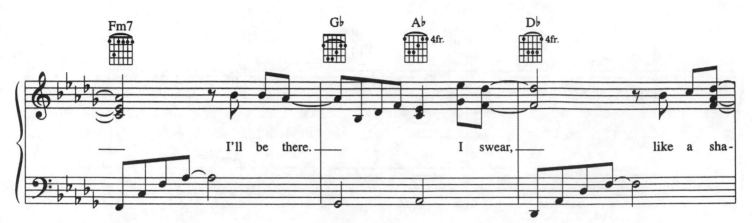

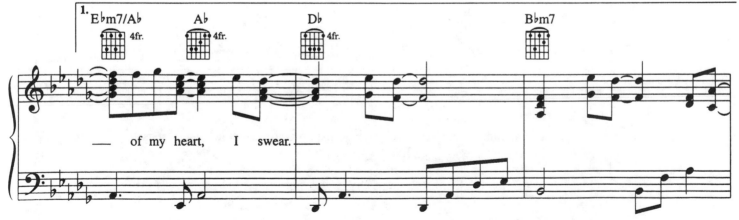

I Swear - 4 - 3

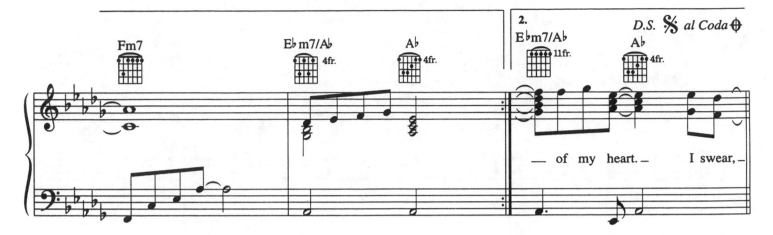

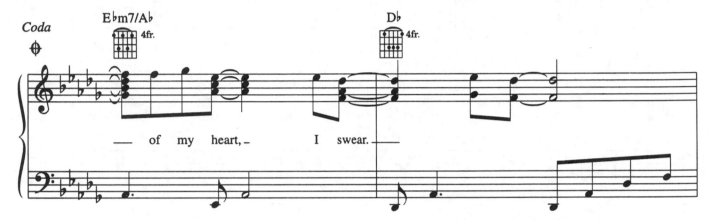

*Additional lyrics*

2.   I'll give you everything I can,
I'll build your dreams with these two hands,
And we'll hang some memories on the wall.
And when there's silver in your hair,
You won't have to ask if I still care,
'Cause as time turns the page my love won't age at all.
*(To Chorus)*

# I THINK ABOUT YOU

Words and Music by
STEVE SESKIN and DON SCHLITZ

I Think about You - 4 - 1

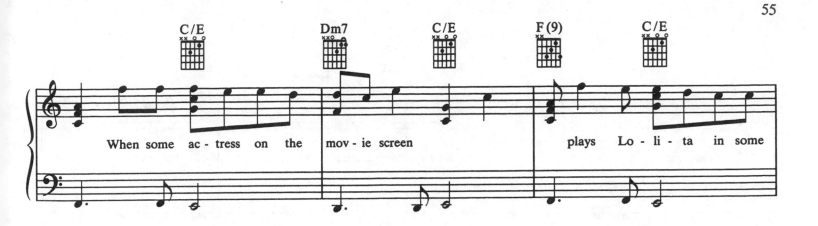

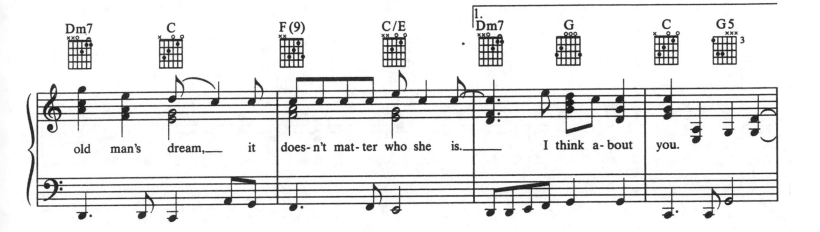

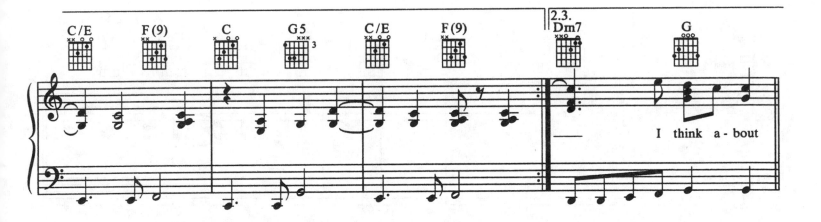

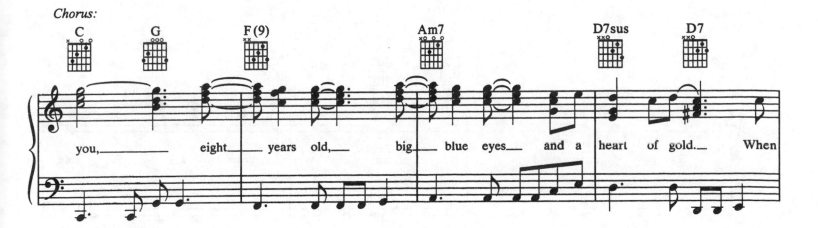

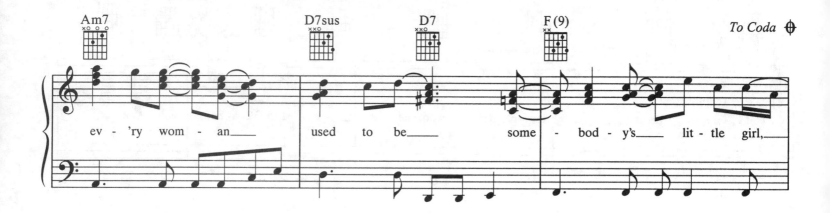

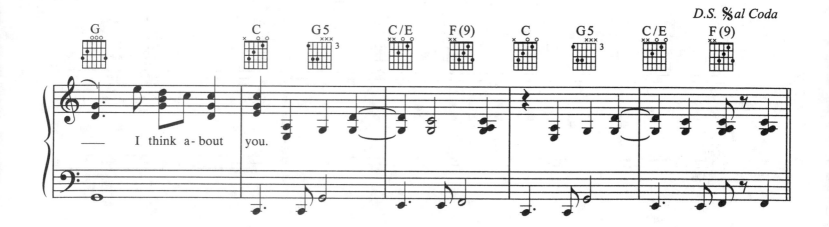

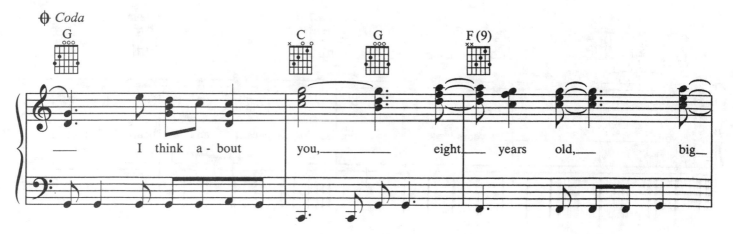

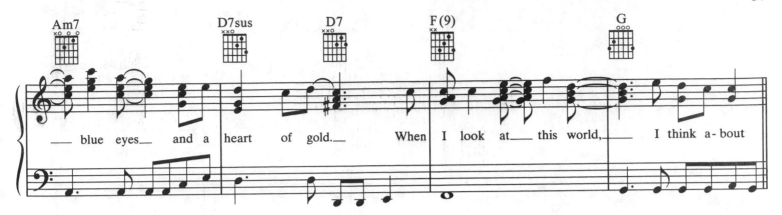

blue eyes___ and a heart of gold.___ When I look at___ this world,___ I think a-bout

*Repeat ad lib. and fade*

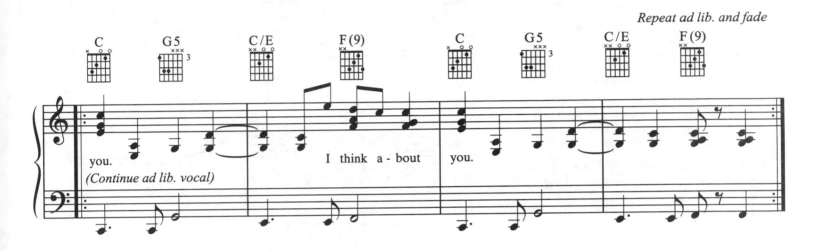

you. I think a-bout you.

*(Continue ad lib. vocal)*

*Verse 2:*
When I see a pretty woman walkin' down the street,
I think about you.
Men look her up and down like she's some kind of tree.
Oh, I think about you.
She wouldn't dare talk to a stranger,
Always has to be aware of the danger,
It doesn't matter who she is,
I think about you.
*(To Chorus:)*

*Verse 3:*
Every time I hear people say it's never gonna change,
I think about you.
Like it's some kind of joke, some kind of game,
Girl, I think about you.
When I see a woman on the news
Who didn't ask to be abandoned or abused,
It doesn't matter who she is,
I think about you.
*(To Chorus:)*

# I'D FALL IN LOVE TONIGHT

Words and Music by
NAOMI MARTIN and
MIKE REID

*Vocal sung one octave lower

I'd Fall in Love Tonight - 3 - 1

I'd Fall in Love Tonight - 3 - 2

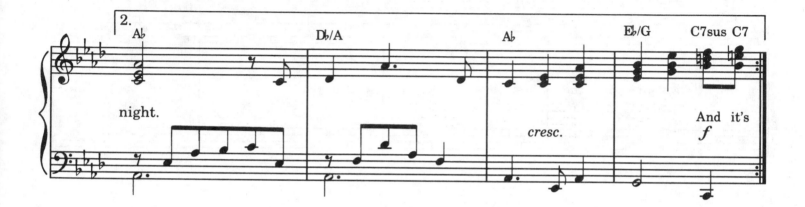

# IF I COULD MAKE A LIVING

Words and Music by
ALAN JACKSON, KEITH STEGALL
and ROGER MURRAH

Moderate country two-beat ♩ = 72

*Chorus:*

If I could make a liv-ing out of

lov-ing you,___ I'd be a mil-lion-aire in a week or two.___ I'd be

do-ing what I love and lov-ing what I do___ if I could make a liv-ing out of

If I Could Make a Living - 5 - 1

62

week or two.__ I'd be do-ing what I love and lov - ing what I do__ if

I could make a liv-ing out of lov - ing__ you.

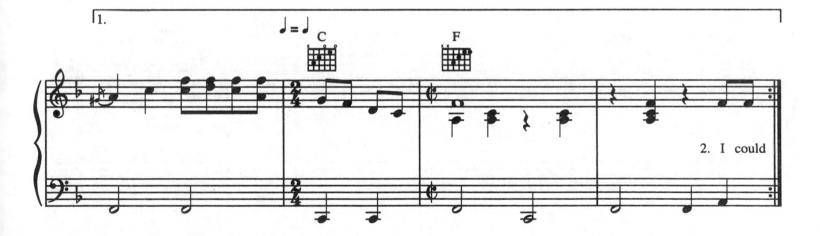

2. I could

*Chorus:*

If I could make a liv-ing out of lov-ing you,— I'd

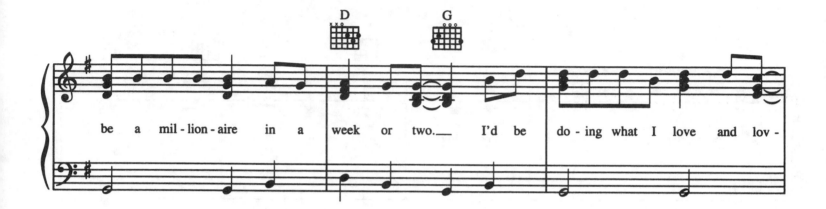

be a mil-lion-aire in a week or two.— I'd be do-ing what I love and lov-

-ing what I do— if I could make a liv-ing out of lov-ing— you. If

*Chorus:*

I could make a liv-ing out of lov-ing you,— I'd be a mil-lion-aire in a

week or two.___ I'd be do - ing what I love and lov - ing what I do___ if

I could make a liv - ing out of lov - ing___ you.

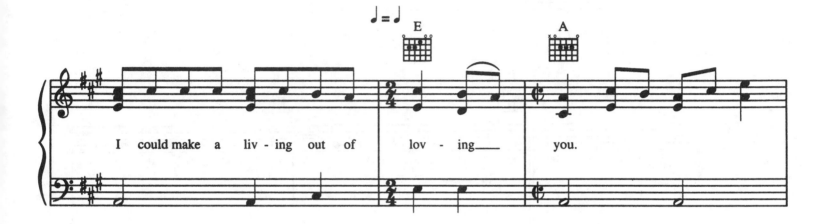

*Verse 2:*
I could work all day and feel right at home
Loving that 8 to 5,
And never have to leave you here alone
When I'm working over-time.
*(To Chorus:)*

# IF THERE HADN'T BEEN YOU

Words and Music by
TOM SHAPIRO and RON SHELLARD

If There Hadn't Been You - 4 - 1

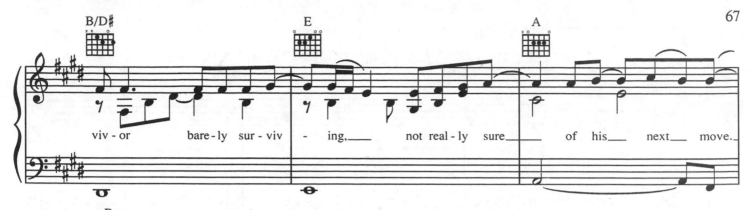

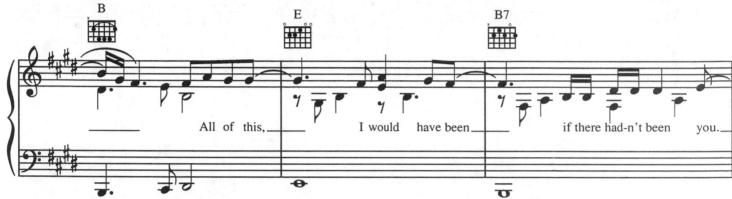

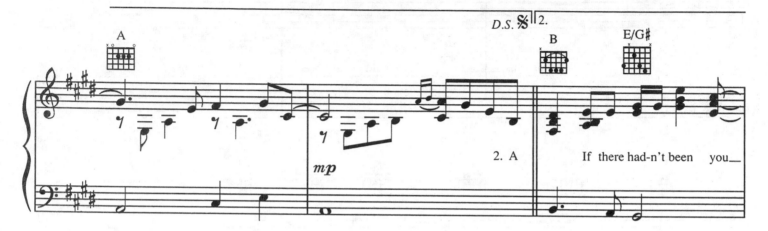

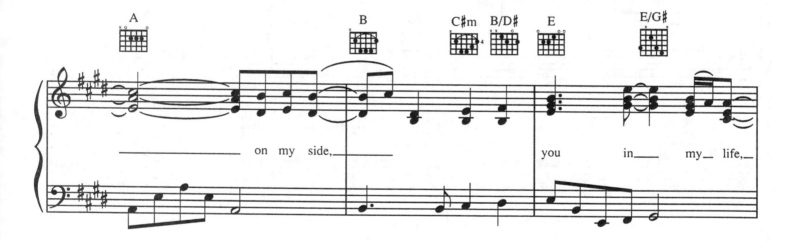

All— my dreams— would still be dreams—

if there had-n't been you.—

rit.

*Verse 2:*
A man filled with hope,
Who finally knows
Where he belongs.
A heart filled with love,
More than enough to keep it strong.
A life that's alive again,
No longer afraid to face the truth.
All of this I would have missed
If there hadn't been you.

# IF TOMORROW NEVER COMES

Words and Music by
KENT BLAZY and GARTH BROOKS

would she ev - er doubt _____ the way _____ I feel _____ a - bout _____ her in _____ my

*Chorus:*

heart. _____   If to - mor - row nev-er comes,   will she know how much I

loved her? _____   Did I try in ev - ery way _____ to show her ev - ery - day _____

_____ that she's my on-ly one? _____   And if my   time on _ earth _ were

through, _   and she must   face _ this world with - out _ me, _____

If Tomorrow Never Comes - 3 - 2

72

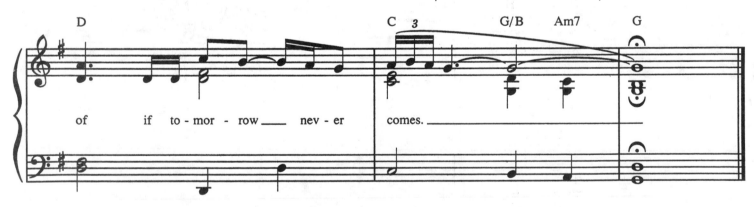

*Verse 2:*
'Cause I've lost loved ones in my life.
Who never knew how much I loved them.
Now I live with the regret
That my true feelings for them never were revealed.
So I made a promise to myself
To say each day how much she means to me
And avoid that circumstance
Where there's no second chance to tell her how I feel. ('Cause)
*(To Chorus:)*

# I'M THE ONLY THING I'LL HOLD AGAINST YOU

Words and Music by
KIM WILLIAMS, JOE DIFFIE
and LONNIE WILSON

I'm the Only Thing I'll Hold Against You - 3 - 1

Verse 2:
I knew it'd be just like the first time that I held you,
When we swore that our love would always last.
Let's give it one more try; don't be afraid to.
Onc touch, and we'll forget about the past.
(To Chorus:)

# IN THIS LIFE

Words and Music by
MIKE REID and
ALLEN SHAMBLIN

In This Life - 3 - 1

With one hon - est touch you set me free.___ Let the

*Chorus:*

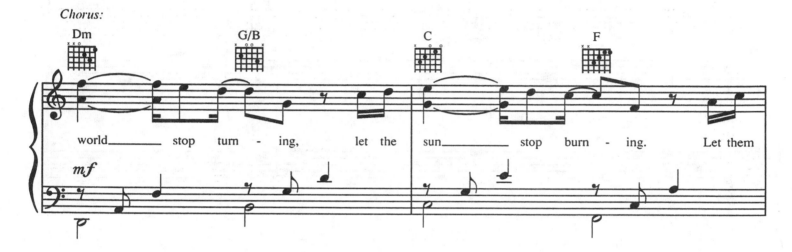

world_____ stop turn - ing, let the sun_____ stop burn - ing. Let them

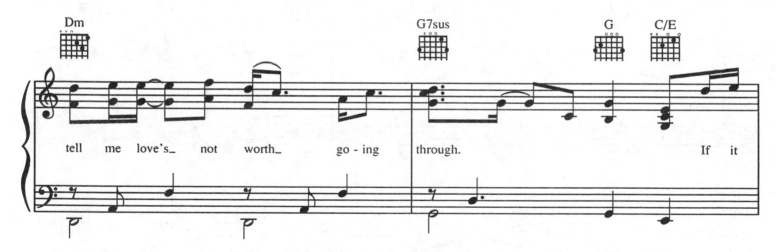

tell me love's_ not worth_ go - ing through. If it

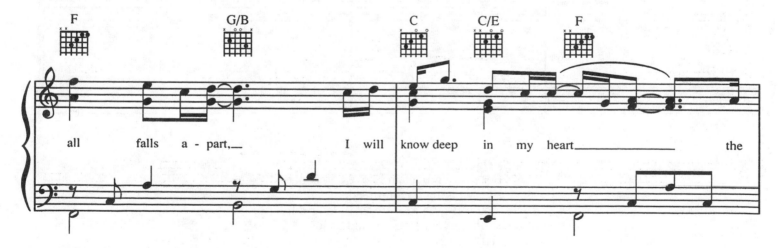

all falls a - part,___ I will know deep in my heart_____ the

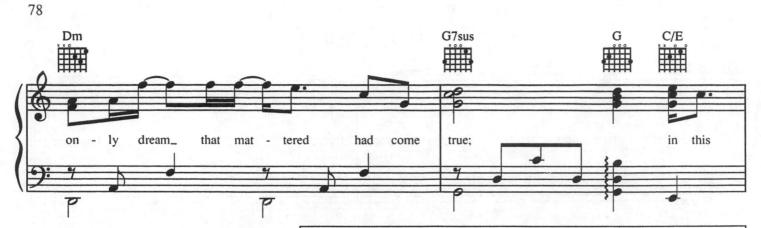

on - ly dream_ that mat - tered had come true; in this

life I was loved_ by you. *dim.* **mp**

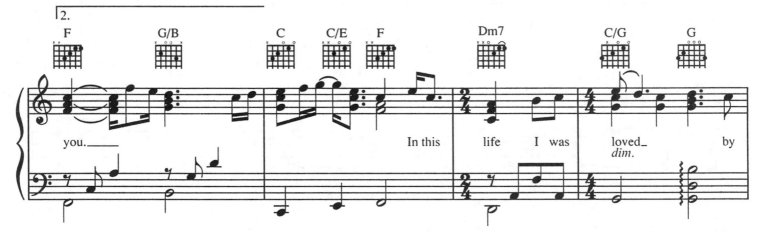

you.___ In this life I was loved_ by
*dim.*

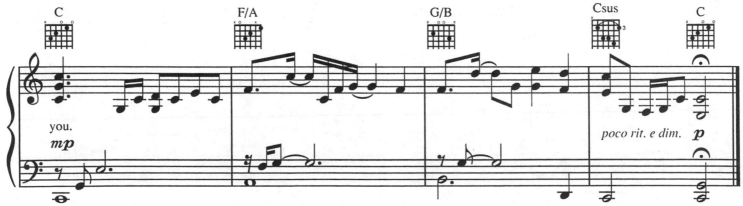

you. *poco rit. e dim.* **p**
**mp**

*Verse 2:*
For every mountain I have climbed.
Every raging river crossed,
You were the treasure that I longed to find.
Without your love I would be lost.
*(To Chorus:)*

# LET ME BE THERE

Words and Music by
JOHN ROSTILL

Let Me Be There - 3 - 1

in ev-'ry-thing you do. _____
you know I'll be there. _____

Let me be_

_____ there in your morn ‐ ing. Let me be _____ there in your night.__

_____ Let me change ___ what - ev -er's wrong _____ and make it right.

Let me take _____ you through that won ‐ der - land _____ that ___

*Let Me Be There - 3 - 2*

on - ly two can share._____ All I ask_____ you _____

to Coda 1. 

_____ is let me be there. _____

2. D.S. al Coda

2. Watch-ing you grow_____ Let me be_____

Coda

All I ask_____ you _____ is let me be there. _____

Let Me Be There - 3 - 3

# I'LL STILL BE LOVING YOU

Words and Music by
PAT BUNCH, PAM ROSE,
MARY ANN KENNEDY and TODD CERNEY

I'll Still Be Loving You - 4 - 1

I'll still be lov - ing, I'll still be lov - ing you.

I'll still be lov - ing— you.

I'll Still Be Loving You - 4 - 4

# THE KEEPER OF THE STARS

Words and Music by
KAREN STALEY, DANNY MAYO and DICKEY LEE

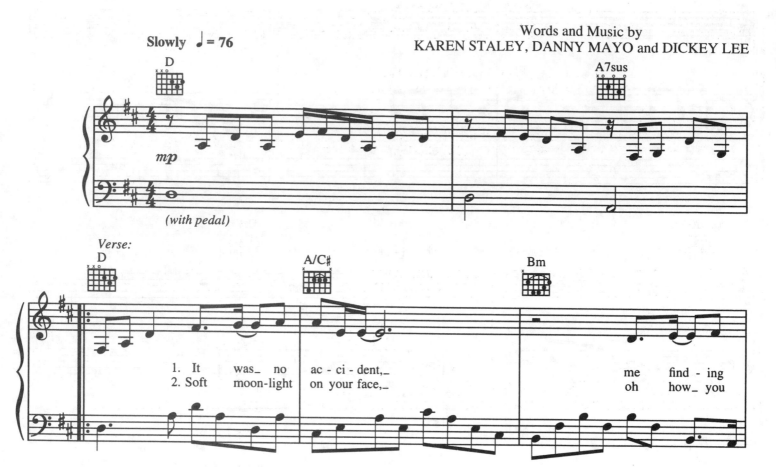

Slowly ♩ = 76

(with pedal)

Verse:

1. It was no ac-ci-dent,_ me find-ing
2. Soft moon-light on your face,_ oh how_ you

you. Some-one had a hand_ in it___
shine! It takes my_ breath_ a-way_

long be-fore_ we_ ev-er___ knew.
just to look_ in-to your___ eyes.

The Keeper of the Stars - 4 - 1

Chorus:

The Keeper of the Stars - 4 - 2

He sure knew what he\_\_ was do - in'\_\_ when he joined these two\_\_

hearts. I hold ev - 'ry - thing

when I hold you in my\_ arms. I've got all I'll ev-er need

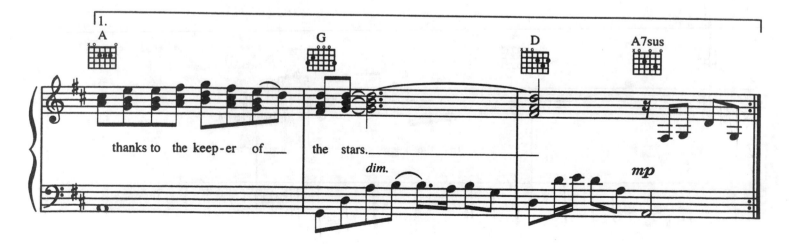

thanks to the keep-er of\_\_ the stars.\_\_

*dim.*

*mp*

thanks to the keep - er of\_\_\_ the stars.\_\_

*dim.*

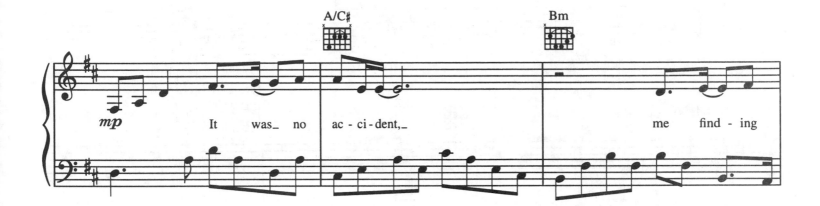

*mp*

It was\_ no ac - ci - dent,\_

me find - ing

you.

Some-one had a hand\_ in it\_\_\_

long be - fore\_ we\_ ev - er knew.

*u tempo*  *dim. e rit.*

*p*

# LIKE A RIVER TO THE SEA

Words and Music by
STEVE WARINER

Like a River to the Sea - 4 - 1

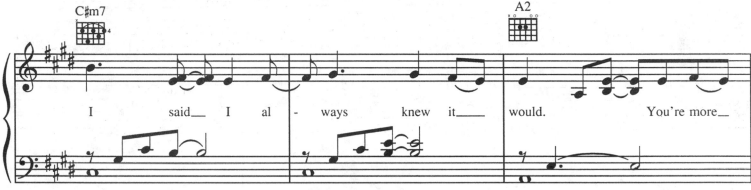

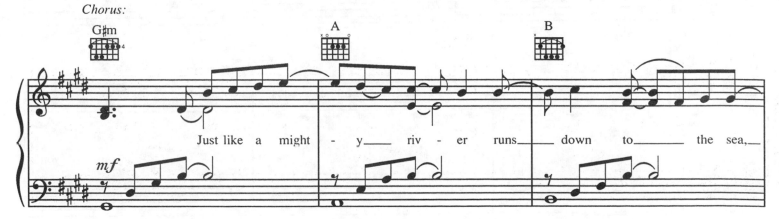

92

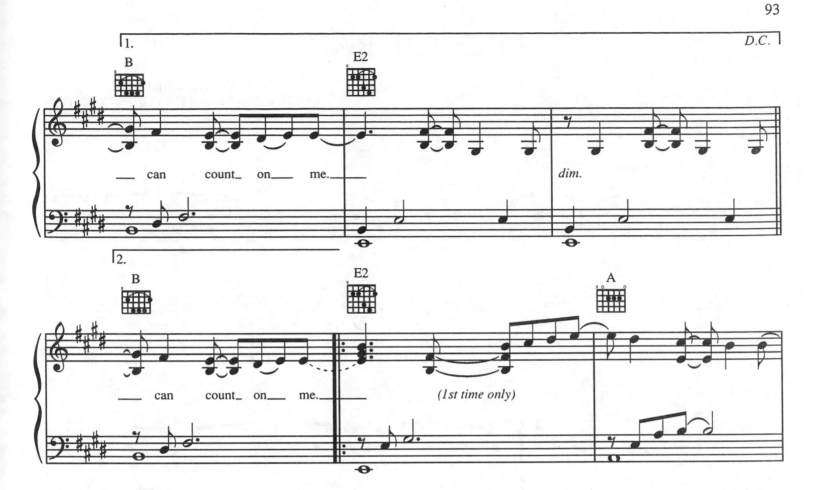

*Verse 2:*
These hands on the clock should know
That time just can't pass this slow
When I am away.
But I've got my job to do.
Then I'll hurry home to you;
I'm always waiting for the day.
*(To Chorus:)*

# LIKE THE RAIN

Words and Music by
CLINT BLACK and HAYDEN NICHOLAS

1. I nev-er liked the rain___ till___ I walked___ through it___ with you.___ Ev-'ry

2.3. *See additional lyrics*

thun-der cloud___ that came___ was one___ more I___ might not___ get through.___ But on the dark-

-est day___ there's al-ways light,___ and now I see___ it, too.___ But I

Like the Rain - 5 - 1

falling for you now,_____ just like the rain.____ I have fall - en for__ you, I'm

fall - ing for you now,_____ just like__ the rain.____ And when the
*decresc.*

*Bridge:*

night falls on our bet - ter days_____ and we're look-in' to the sky_____ for the
*mf*

winds to take us high_____ a-bove the plains,____ I know that we'll__ find bet-ter ways___

*Verse 2:*
I hear it falling in thc night and filling up my mind.
All the heavens' rivers come to light and I see it all unwind.
I hear it talking through the trees and on the window pane,
And when I hear it, I just can't believe I never liked the rain.
*(To Chorus:)*

*Verse 3:*
When the cloud is rolling over, thunder striking me,
It's as bright as lightning and I wonder why I couldn't see
That it's always good and when the flood is gone we still remain.
Guess I've known all along I just belong here with you falling...
*(To Chorus:)*

# LONG AS I LIVE

Words and Music by
RICK BOWLES and
WILL ROBINSON

Long As I Live - 5 - 1

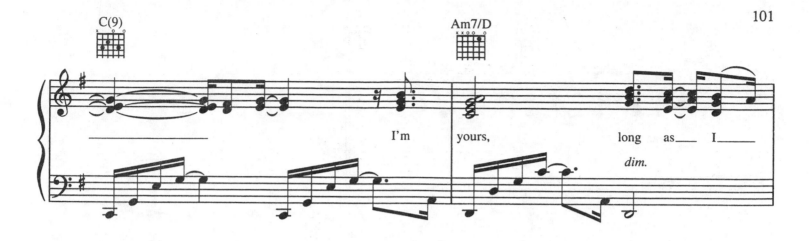

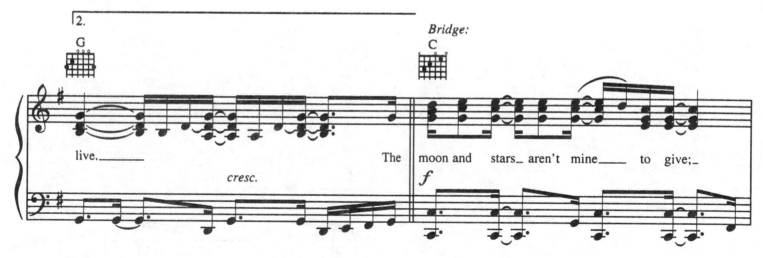

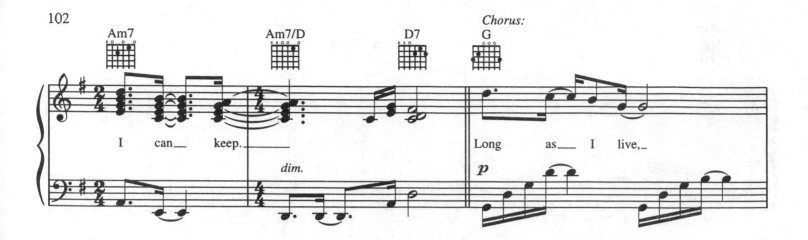

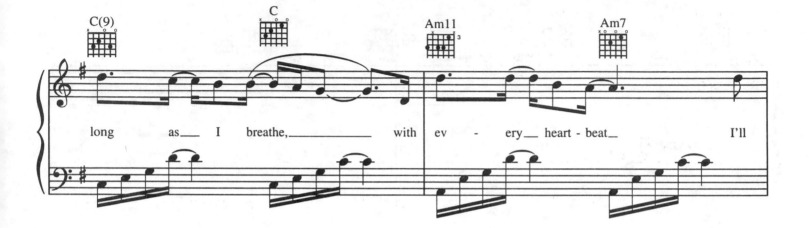

I'm          yours long__ as I_ live._____          I'm

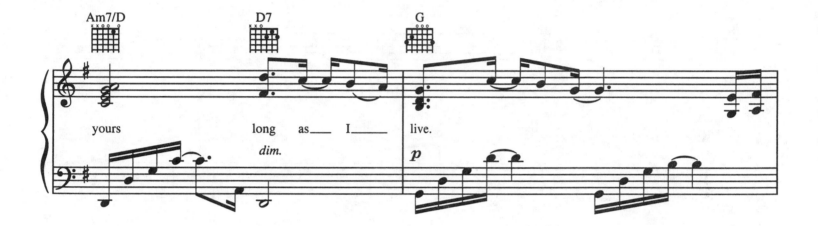

yours          long as__ I____ live.          *dim.*          *p*

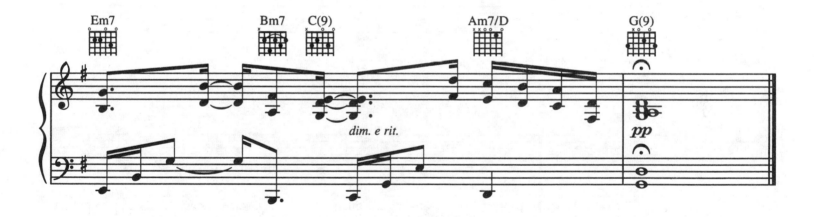

*dim. e rit.*          *pp*

*Verse 2:*
No matter if there are mountains you can't move,
Or harder times than you thought you'd go through,
When the weight of your world's too much to bear,
Just remember I'll always be there.
*(To Chorus:)*

# LIVIN' ON LOVE

Words and Music by
ALAN JACKSON

**Moderately**

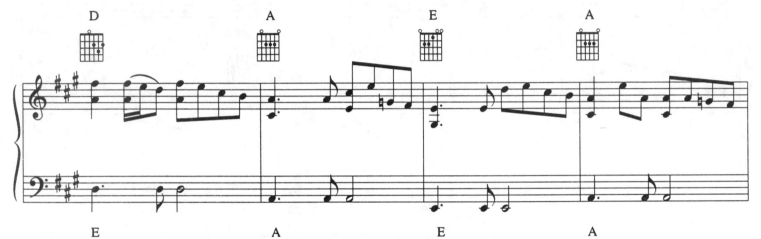

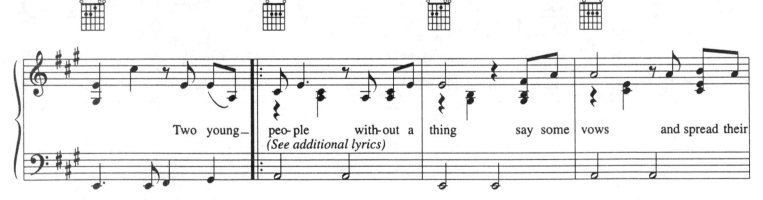

Two young— peo- ple with-out a thing say some vows and spread their
*(See additional lyrics)*

wings.— And set- tle down— with just— what they need— liv- in' on love.—

Livin' on Love - 4 - 1

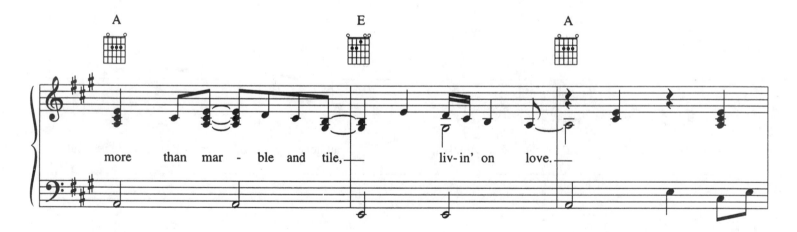

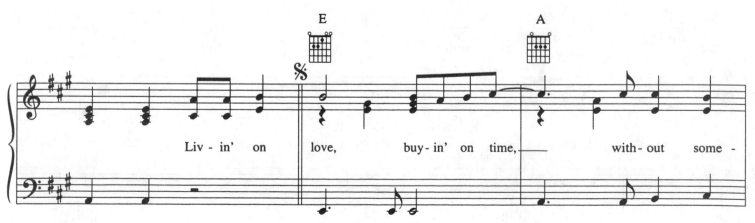

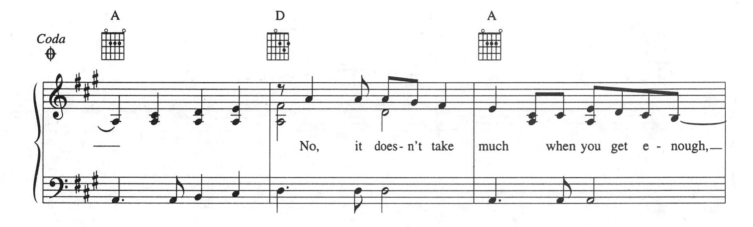

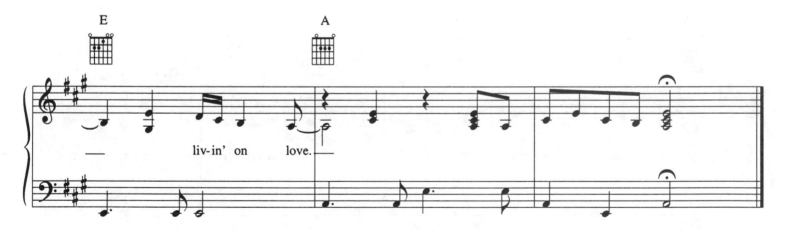

*Additional Lyrics*

2. Two old people without a thing
   Children gone but still they sing
   Side by side in that front porch swing
   Livin' on love.
   He can't see anymore,
   She can barely sweep the floor.
   Hand in hand they'll walk through that door
   Just livin' on love.
   *(To Chorus)*

# MY LOVE

Written by
PORTER HOWELL, BRADY SEALS
and TOMMY BARNES

Moderate country rock ♩ = 92

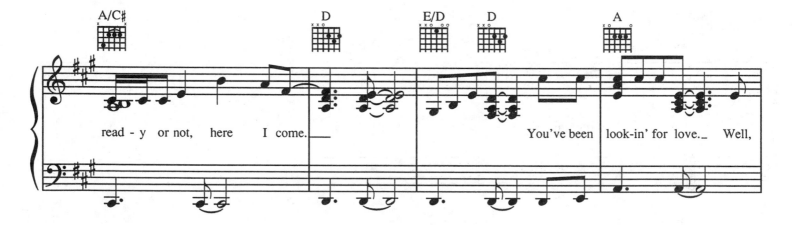

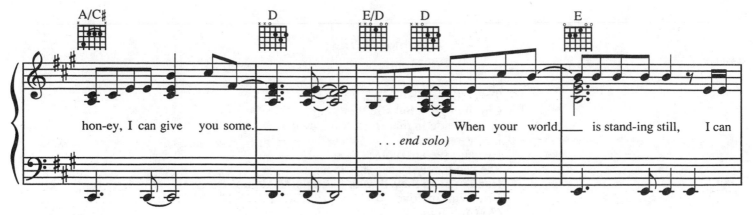

My Love - 4 - 1

My Love - 4 - 2

my love is read - y for you. _____ *mf*

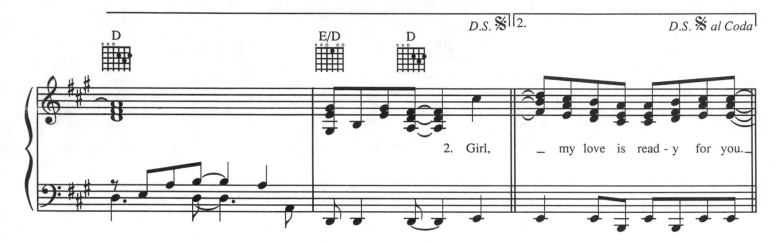

2. Girl, _ my love is read - y for you. _

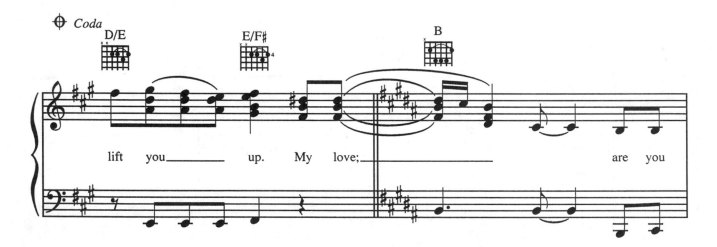

lift you _____ up. My love; _____ are you

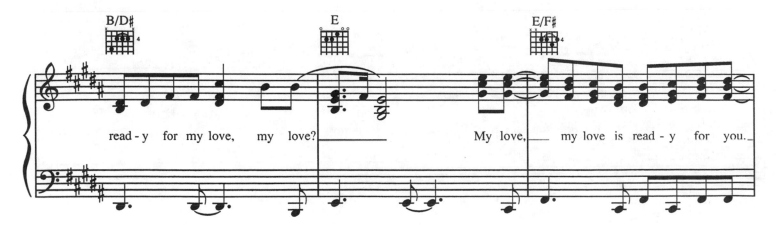

read - y for my love, my love? _____ My love, _ my love is read - y for you. _

If you're look-in' for a heart_ that's al - ways_ true_ on - ly to you,_

_ then my love,_ my love,_ my love is read-y for you._

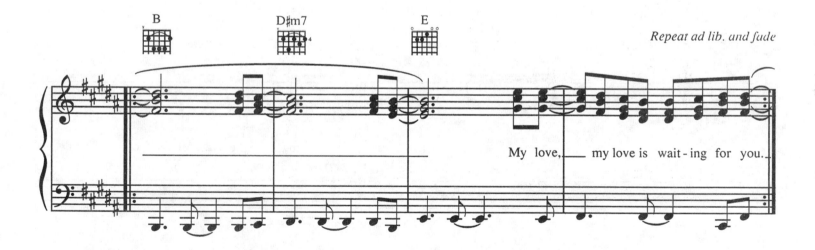

*Repeat ad lib. and fade*

My love,_ my love is wait-ing for you.

*Verse 2:*
Girl, I've heard it said
That love is food for the soul.
I see the hunger in your eyes
Burnin' out of control.
My love is overflowin' from a lovin' cup.
Girl, I know you're down,
But love will lift you up.
*(To Chorus:)*

*Verse 3:*
*(Measures 1-8 Inst. solo ad. lib.)*
My love is overflowin' from a lovin' cup.
Girl, I know you're down,
But love will lift you up.
*(To Coda)*

# NOT A MOMENT TOO SOON

Words and Music by
WAYNE PERRY and
JOE BARNHILL

Slowly ♩ = 60

1. I was stand-ing____ at the end of____ my

rain - bow,____ but no - where to go____ and no____ heart of gold____ in sight.

Not a Moment Too Soon - 4 - 1

All my wish - es___ were just way too much___ to

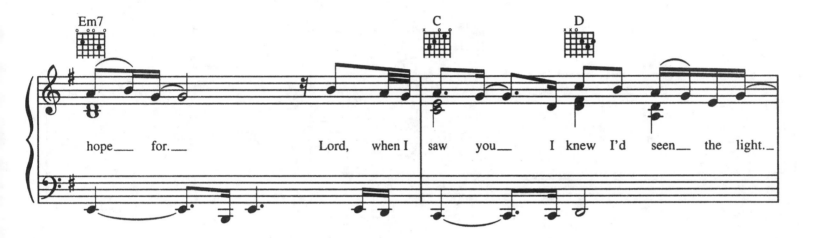

hope___ for.___ Lord, when I saw you___ I knew I'd seen___ the light.___

**(Double time)** ♩ = 120

*Chorus:*

cresc.

And not a mo - ment too___ soon,___ *mf*

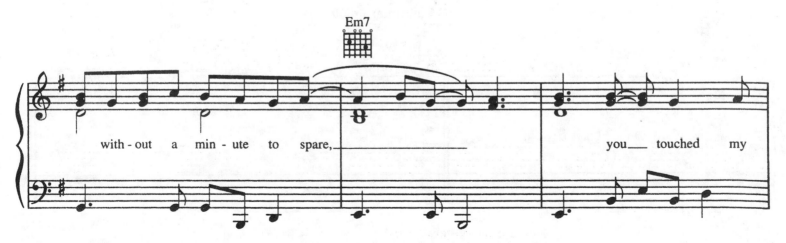

with - out a min - ute to spare,___ you___ touched my

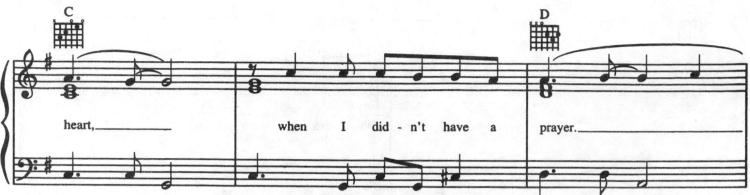

heart,_____ when I did-n't have a prayer._____

_____ In my dark-est hour,_____ with my world_ filled with

gloom._____ Your_ sweet love saved_____

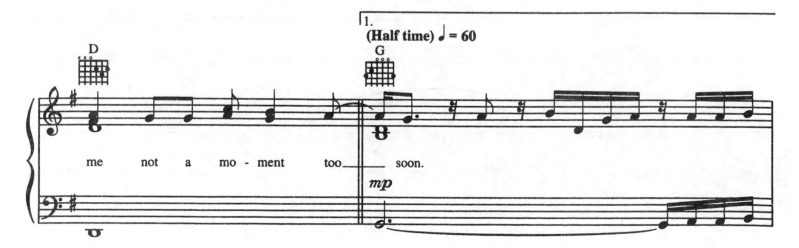

me not a mo-ment too____ soon.

*Verse 2:*
I used to think that love would never find me,
And the one who cares was lost somewhere in time.
But when you found me I knew I'd found forever,
You rescued me just before I crossed the line.
*(To Chorus:)*

# NOW AND FOREVER (YOU AND ME)

a/k/a You And Me (Now And Forever)

Words and Music by
DAVID FOSTER, JIM VALLANCE
and RANDY GOODRUM

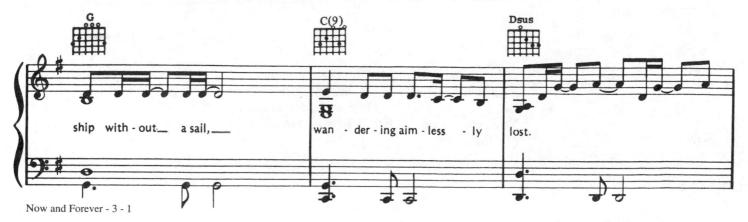

Now and Forever - 3 - 1

tell _____ me there's a heav - en up ___ a -bove, _____ then

that's what I'll be - lieve, ___ 'cause you're the one thing that I'm _____ so sure ___ of. *(Inst. solo ad lib. . . .*

. . . . *end solo)* 3. I feel you

*Verse 2:*
Darlin', inside your eyes, I can see mysteries there.
And you're melting the ice surrounding me;
I'm no longer scared.
I feel you inside my soul, and I'm captured tonight.
But don't let go; this is paradise. *(To Chorus:)*

*Verse 3:*
I feel you inside my soul, and I'm captured tonight.
But don't let go; this is paradise. *(To Chorus:)*

# ONE FRIEND

Words and Music by
DAN SEALS

One Friend - 3 - 1

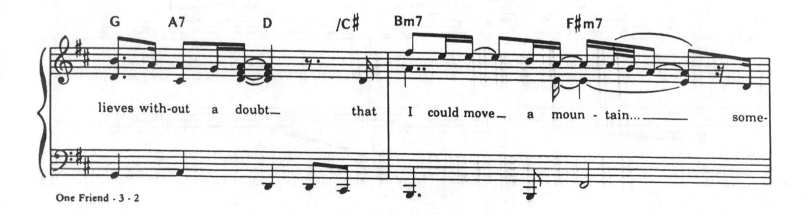

One Friend - 3 - 2

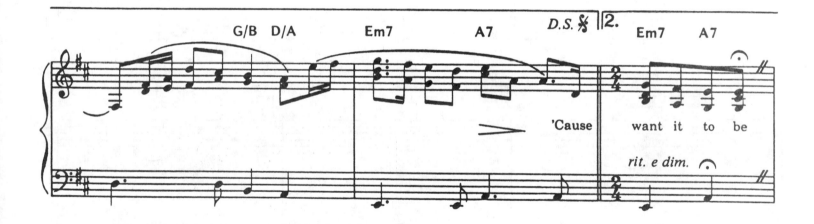

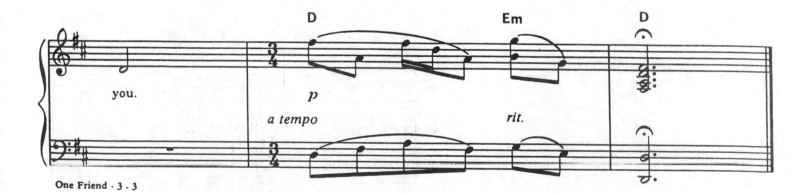

One Friend - 3 - 3

# ONLY LOVE

Words and Music by
ROGER MURRAH and MARCUS HUMMON

Only Love - 3 - 1

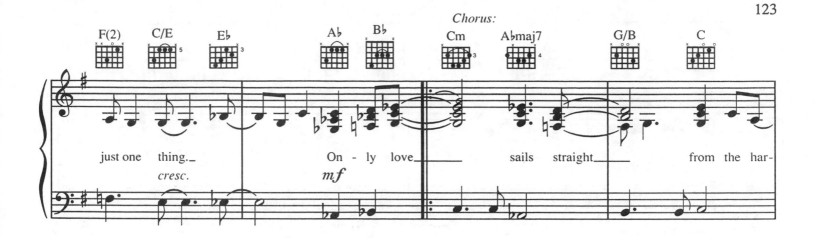

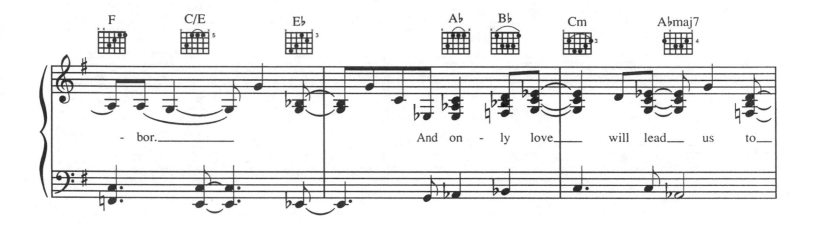

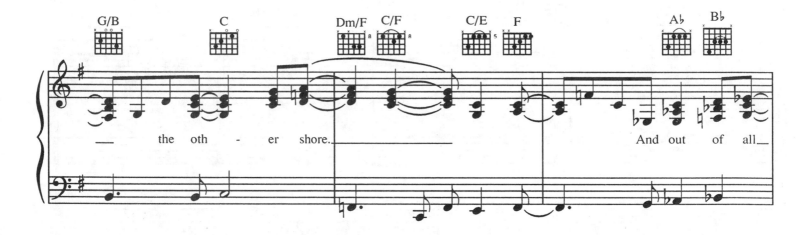

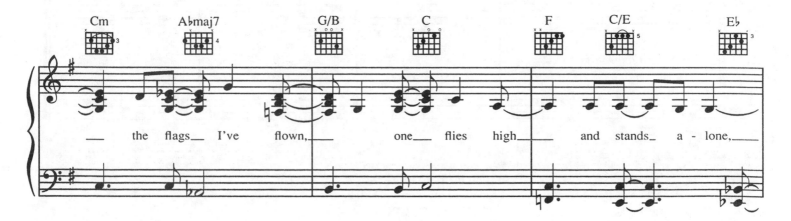

Only Love - 3 - 2

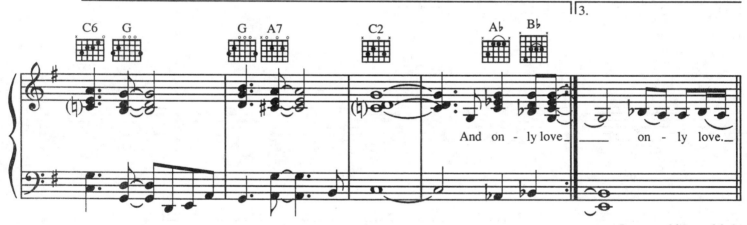

*Verse 2:*
Peaceful waters, raging sea,
It is all the same to me.
I can close my eyes and still be free.
When the waves come crashing down
And thunder rolls around,
I can feel my feet on solid ground.
*(To Chorus:)*

# PRECIOUS THING

Words and Music by
STEVE WARINER and
MAC McANALLY

Precious Thing - 3 - 1

*Verse:*

— 1. In the mid-dle of hard __ times, __ not to men-tion these

*Instr. solo 2nd time . . .*

good times, __ you make me feel __ like a man __ ain't nev-er seen noth-in' but

sun - shine. __ You're the one I come home __ to. __

Girl, you know I still want to! __ When I'm gone, __ no mat-ter how

*To Coda* ⊕ | 1. | 2. *D.S.* 𝄋 *al Coda*

long, you're on __ my mind. __ Ba - by, your 3. If our bills are paid

Baby, your love _____ is a precious thing, _____ Like a new-found home, _____ Like a diamond ring. Nobody knows _____ what tomorrow brings; _ I know your love _____ is a precious thing. _

_ I know your love _____ is a precious thing. _____

Verse 2:
(Inst. solo ad lib.)

Verse 3:
If our bills are paid on time,
Or if we let 'em get way behind,
I still feel like you and me
Are just sittin' on a goldmine.
What more could I ask for.
Honey I'll never be poor,
'Cause I own the world,
As long as you're here by my side.
(To Chorus:)

# ROCKIN' YEARS

Words and Music by
FLOYD PARTON

Rockin' Years - 3 - 1

129

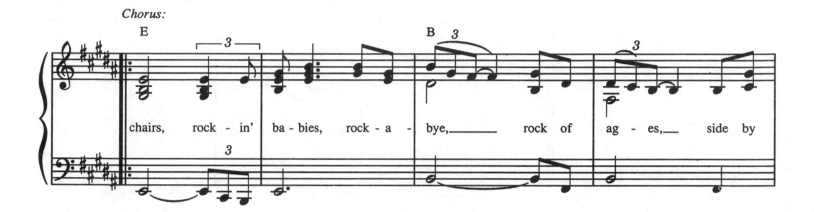

Rockin' Years - 3 - 2

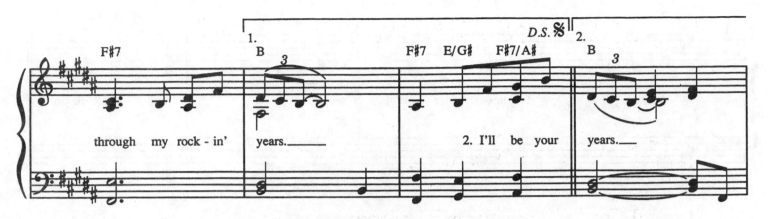

*Verse 2:*
I'll be your friend, I'll be your lover,
Until the end, there'll be no other,
And my heart has only room for one.
Yes, I'll always love you, and I'll always be here for you.
And I'll stand by you through our rockin' years.
*(To Chorus:)*

# SHE DON'T KNOW SHE'S PERFECT

Words and Music by
JERRY LYNN WILLIAMS, DAVID BELLAMY
and HOWARD BELLAMY

**Moderate rock** ♩ = 108

*mf*

*with pedal*

1. Your brok- en heart's_ been fad-

sweet- est thing_ you've ev-

*Verse:*

-ing fast._ You've fin- 'lly found_ a love_

-er seen,_ the kind of girl_ that's al-

_ you think_ will last._

-ways in_ your dreams,_

1.3.5.6.

and last._

She Don't Know She's Perfect - 3 - 1

The ____ in your

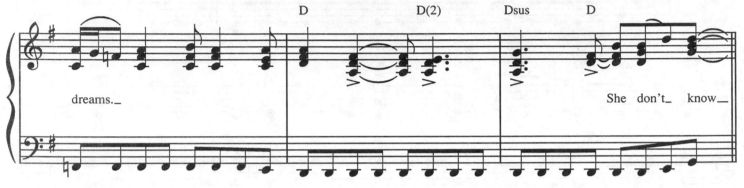

dreams.____ She don't____ know____

*Chorus:*

that she's per - fect.____

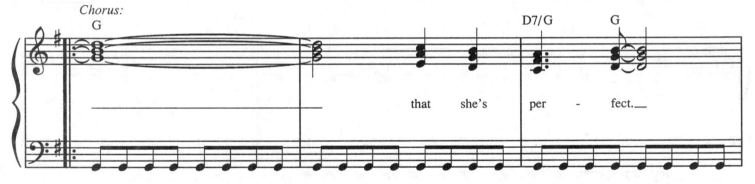

She does not have____ a clue____
Bet-ter find the words____ to say,____

what she's done____ to you.____ She don't____ know____ don't let her walk____ a - way.____

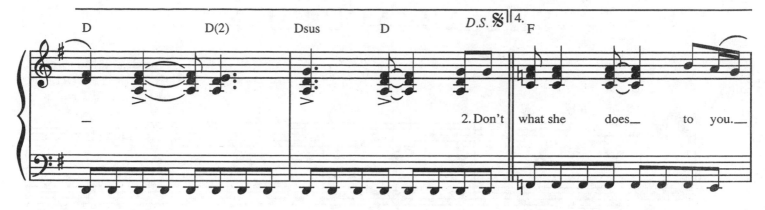

*Verse 2:*
Don't get me wrong, don't think me strange,
There's nothin' about you, girl, I'd want to change.
I'd never change you.
But the day has come and now's the time,
I'll find a way to make you say you're mine,
Mine, all mine.
*Chorus 2:*
She don't know that she's perfect.
You'd better let her know
Before she turns to go.
*Verse 3:*
*Instrumental solo*
*Verse 4:*
I hope and pray she'll understand
That one fine day I just might be her man,
Be her man.
We'll find a place down in the sun,
Where she and I can live as one, my friend
Till the end.
*Chorus 3:*
She don't know that she's perfect.
She does not have a clue
What she does to you.

# STAND BY YOUR MAN

Words and Music by
TAMMY WYNETTE and
BILLY SHERRILL

Stand By Your Man - 2 - 1

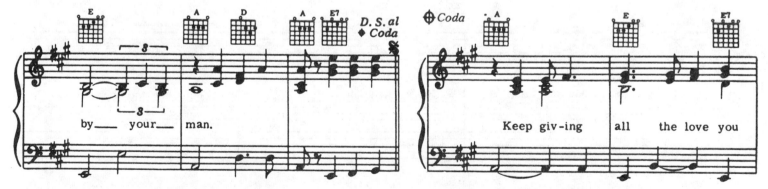

Stand By Your Man - 2 - 2

# THEY'RE PLAYIN' OUR SONG

Words and Music by
BOB DIPIERO, JOHN JARRARD
and MARK D. SANDERS

Moderately ♩ = 88

*Verse 1:*

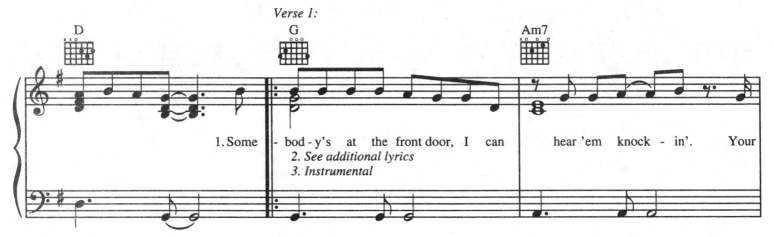

1. Some - bod - y's at the front door, I can hear 'em knock - in'. Your
2. *See additional lyrics*
3. *Instrumental*

ma - ma's on the phone___ and she feels like talk - in'. There's chick - en on the bar - be - cue

bar - be - cue - in'. Don't wor - ry 'bout it, ba - by, just drop what you're do - in'. 'Cause they're

They're Playin' Our Song - 4 - 1

*Chorus:*

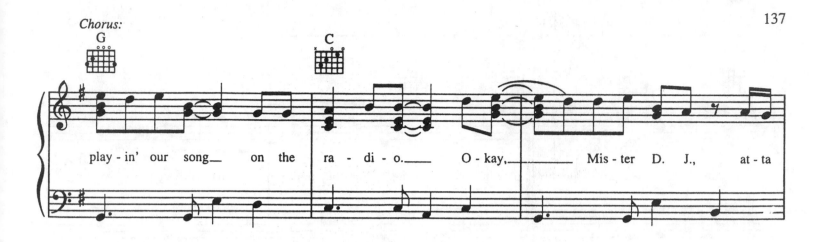

play - in' our song___ on the ra - di - o.___ O - kay,___ Mis - ter D. J., at - ta

way to go.___ A mil - lion watts of love___ pow - er com - in' on strong.___ Dance___

___ with me dar - lin', they're play - in' our___ song.___

2. Oh the

play-in' our___ song.___ | play-in' our___ song. Oh, they're play - in' our song___ on the

ra - di - o.___ O-kay,___ Mis - ter D. J., at - ta way to go.___ A mil-

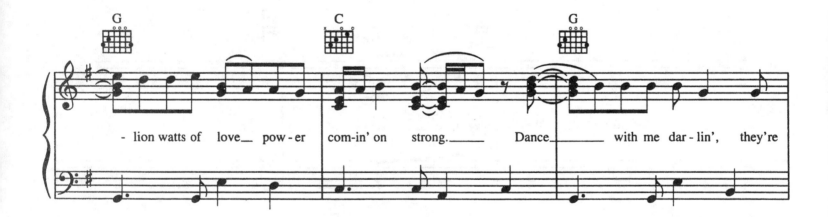

- lion watts of love___ pow - er com-in' on strong.___ Dance___ with me dar - lin', they're

play-in' our___ song.___

Repeat ad lib. and fade

*Verse 2:*
Oh, the house needs cleanin', the grass needs mowin',
We both got places that we need to be goin'.
Tomorrow's a big day, better get ready,
But tonight it's just you and me rockin' steady.
*(To Chorus:)*

# THINKIN' ABOUT YOU

Moderately ♩ = 92

Words and Music by
TOM SHAPIRO and BOB REGAN

Verse 1:

1. I'm not quite sure what's go-in' on, but all day through and

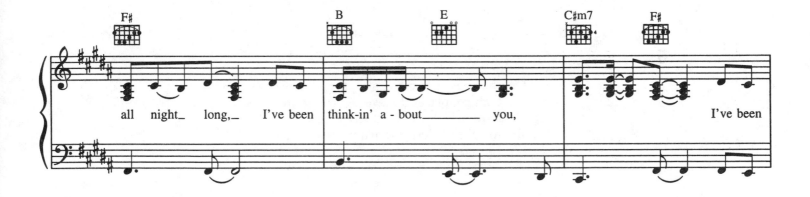

all night long, I've been think-in' a-bout you, I've been

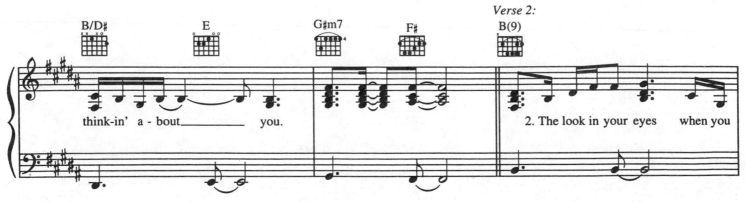

think-in' a-bout you. 2. The look in your eyes when you

Thinkin' about You - 4 - 1

smile that way,___ the sound of your voice say - in' my name.___ I've been

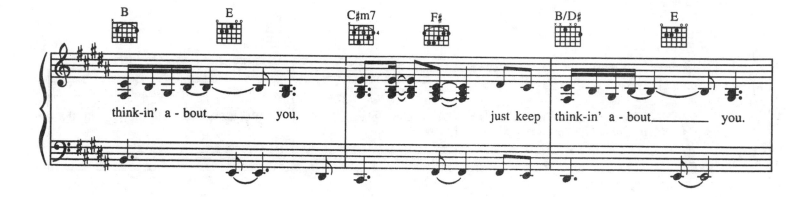

think-in' a - bout_____ you, just keep think-in' a - bout_____ you.

𝄋 *Bridge:*

This sin - gle - mind - ed fas - ci - na - tion I've got,___

do you call it love? If you don't, then what? All I know is I don't know___

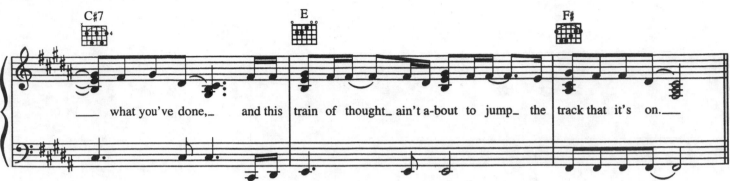

*Verses 3 & 4:*

3. In the back of my mind, there's a se - cret place._ But the whole world knows by the

smile on my face_ that I've been think-in' a-bout_ you.

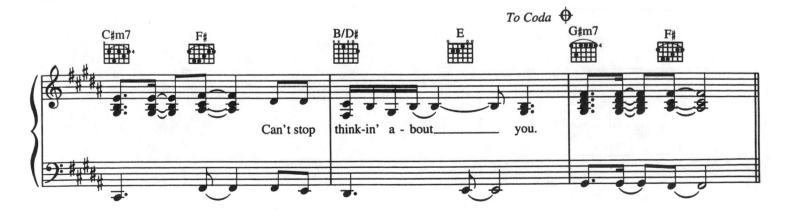

Can't stop think-in' a-bout_ you.

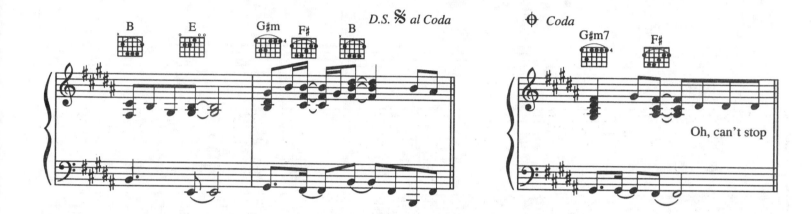

*Verse 4:*
I know it's crazy, callin' you this late,
When the only thing I wanted to say is that
I've been thinkin' about you,
Oh, just keep thinkin' about you.

# TWO HEARTS

Words and Music by
BOB PARR

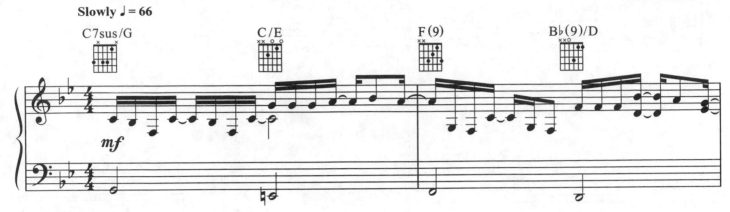

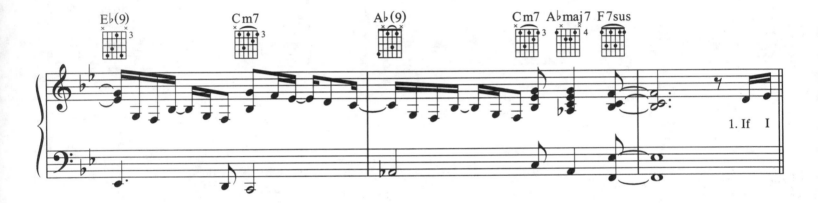

1. If I

had the words_ to make_ you stay_ for - ev - er,_   I would form them ev - er - y night_ in - to
2. *See additional lyrics*

a_ prayer.   If they   take you by_ sur - prise,_ ev - ery   ef - fort to_ dis - guise_ their mean - ing

Two Hearts - 4 - 1

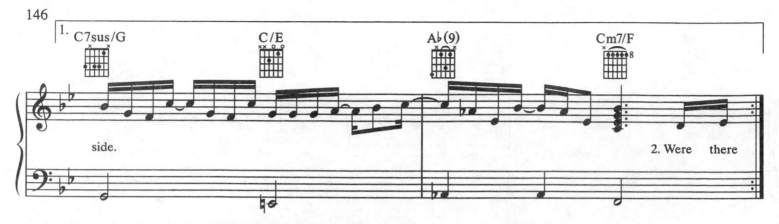

side.                                                                    2. Were there

stay.

When

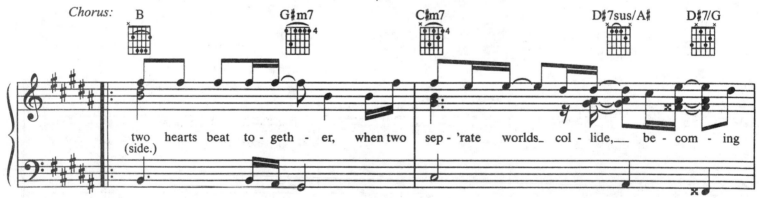

Chorus:

two hearts beat to-geth - er,   when two   sep - 'rate worlds_ col - lide,_ be - com - ing
(side.)

one,   our   love_ will sur - vive.        All the   slings and bro - ken ar - rows could-n't

*Verse 2:*
Were there times you thought you had no more to give me?
Were there times you thought you had to walk away?
Did you see me standing there?
Did the feeling catch you unaware,
Remembering the good times that we shared?
Ooh, when I face eternity,
Or the love that set my heart free,
I'll never turn away, I know you're here to stay.
*(To Chorus:)*

# TO ME

Slowly and expressively ♩ = 69

Words and Music by
MACK DAVID and
MIKE REID

To me, you are the hand that I reach for
me, you are the truth I be-lieve in;

when I've lost my way. To me, you are the
I be-lieve in you. To me, you are the

first star of eve-ning, the sun that warms my day.
love I have looked for my whole life through.}

Just as

To Me - 3 - 1

# TWO OF A KIND, WORKIN' ON A FULL HOUSE

A    D    G    E7    A7

Words and Music by
DENNIS ROBBINS, BOBBY BOYD
and WARREN DALE HAYNES

1. Yeah, she's_____ my la-dy luck, hey I'm her

wild card man.___ To-geth-er we're build-in' up a real hot hand.___ We live___

___ out in the coun-try. Hey, she's my lit-tle queen of the south.___

Two of a Kind, Workin' on a Full House - 3 - 1

A

Yeah, we're two of a kind,___ work-in' on___ a full

1.
D

house.

2.3.
D

2. She wakes___ house.

1. Yeah, a pick-

*Bridge:*
G

- up truck___ is her lim-ou-sine.___ And her fa-vor-ite dress is her

D

E7

fad-ed blue jeans.___ She loves me ten - der when the go-in' gets tough.___ Some-times___

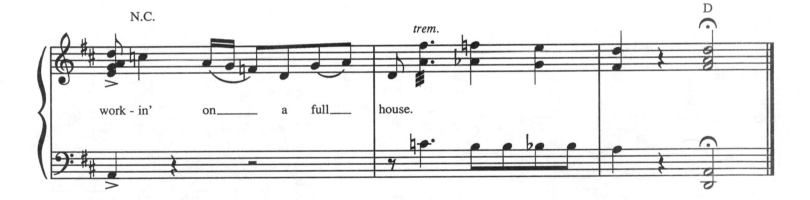

**Verse 2:**
She wakes me every mornin'
With a smile and a kiss.
Her strong country lovin' is hard to resist.
She's my easy lovin' woman,
I'm her hard-workin' man, no doubt.
Yeah, we're two of a kind
Workin' on a full house. *(To Bridge:)*

**Verse 3:**
Lord, I need that little woman
Like the crops need rain.
She's my honeycomb, and I'm her sugar cane.
We really fit together
If you know what I'm talkin' about.
Yeah, we're two of a kind
Workin' on a full house. *(To Bridge 2:)*

**Bridge 2:**
This time I found a keeper, I made up my mind.
Lord, the perfect combination is her heart and mine.
The sky's the limit, no hill is too steep.
We're playin' for fun, but we're playin' for keeps.

**Verse 4:**
So draw the curtain, honey.
Turn the lights down low.
We'll find some country music on the radio.
I'm yours and you're mine.
Hey, that's what it's all about.
Yeah, we're two of a kind
Workin' on a full house.
Lordy mama, we'll be two of a kind
Workin' on a full house.

# SURROUND ME WITH LOVE

Words and Music by
WAYLAND HOLYFIELD and
NORRIS D. WILSON

Surround Me With Love - 3 - 1

# YEARS FROM HERE

Words and Music by
GARY BAKER, JERRY WILLIAMS
and FRANK J. MYERS

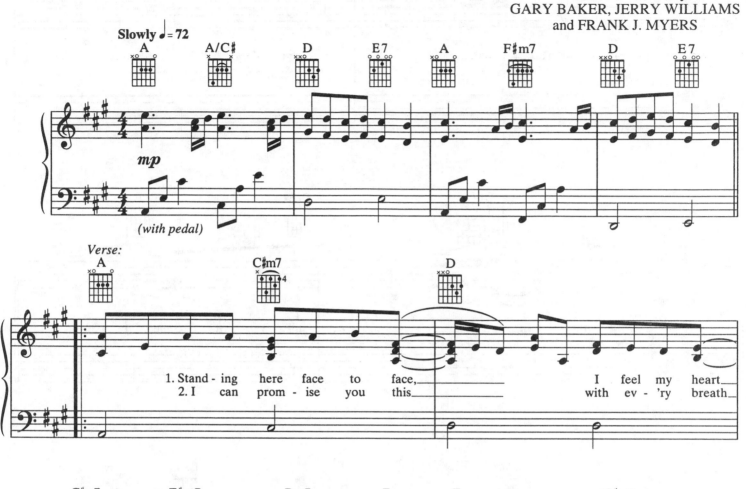

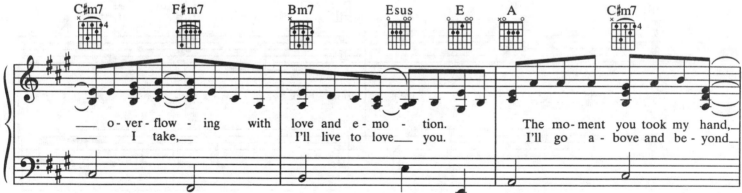

Years from Here - 3 - 1

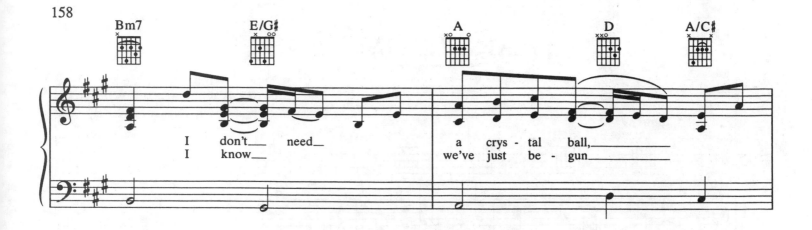

I don't___ need___ a crys - tal ball,_____
I know___ we've just be - gun_____

through your eyes_____ is I see it all.___
*cresc.* and the best_____ is still yet to come.___ }

%S *Chorus:*

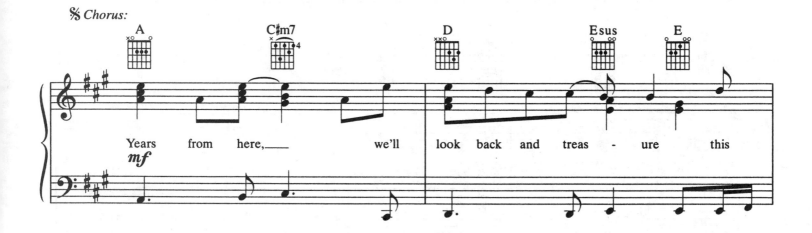

Years from here,___ we'll look back and treas - ure this
*mf*

mo - ment for - ev - er in - side_____ our hearts.___ And from here___

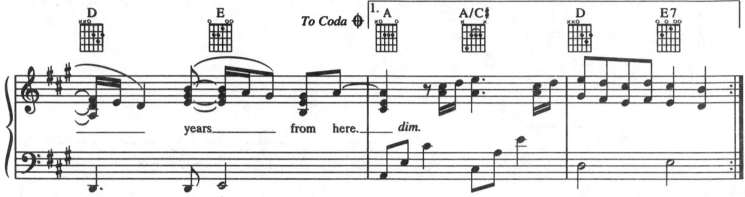

Years from Here - 3 - 3

# WHEN LOVE FINDS YOU

By VINCE GILL
and MICHAEL OMARTIAN

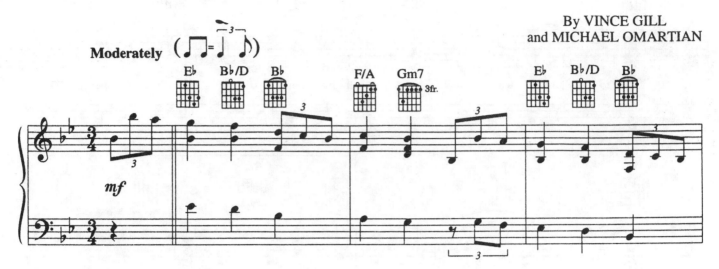

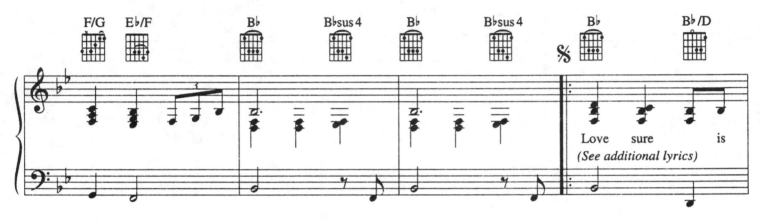

Love sure is
(See additional lyrics)

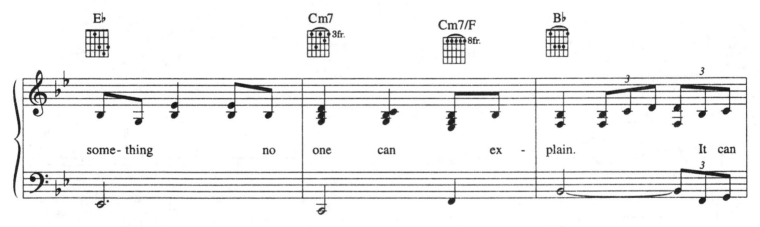

some- thing     no     one     can     ex -     plain.     It     can

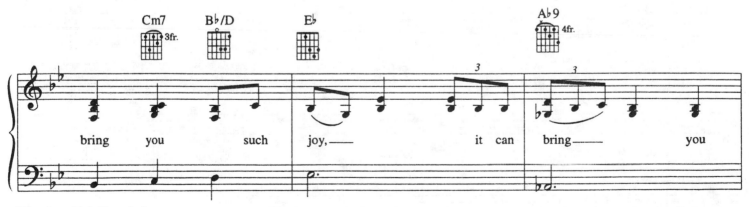

bring     you     such     joy, ——     it     can     bring ——     you

When Love Finds You - 4 - 1

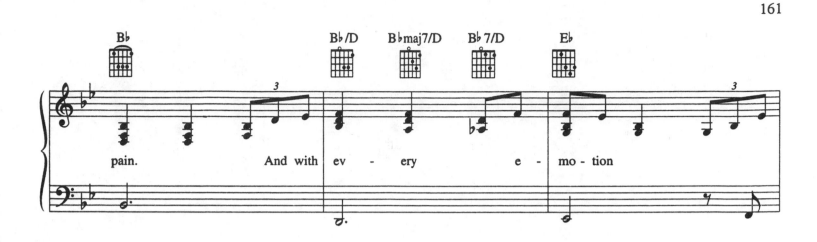

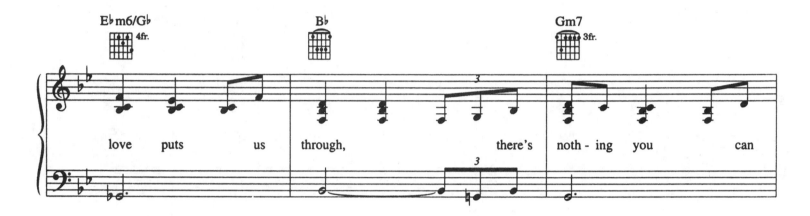

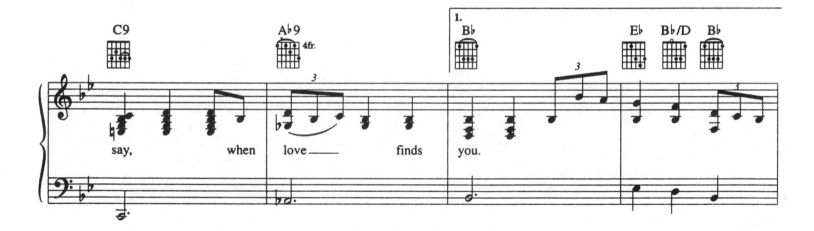

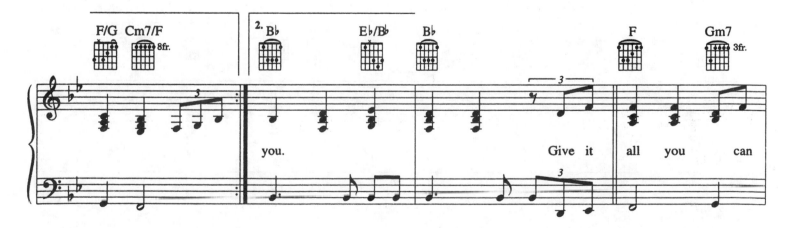

When Love Finds You - 4 - 2

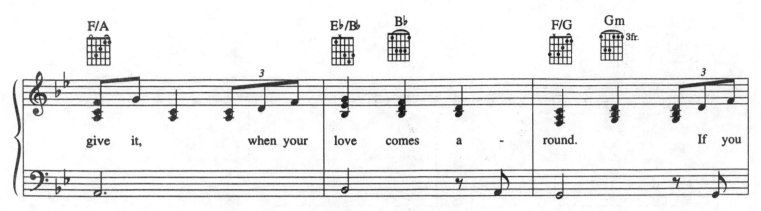

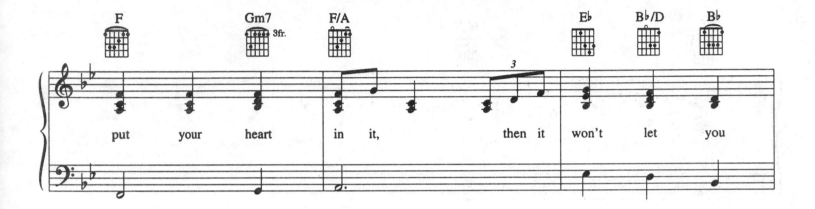

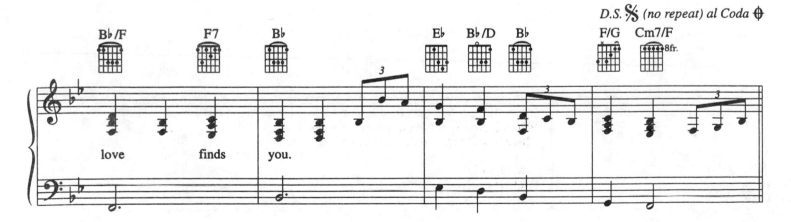

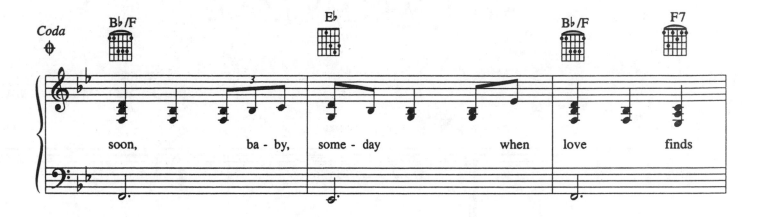

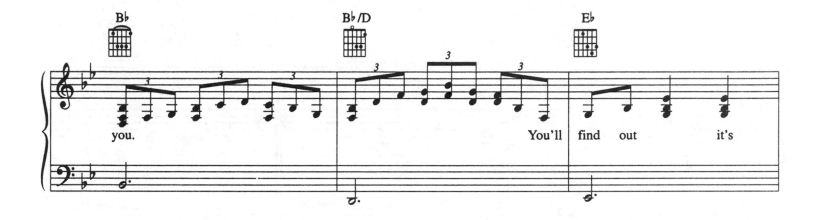

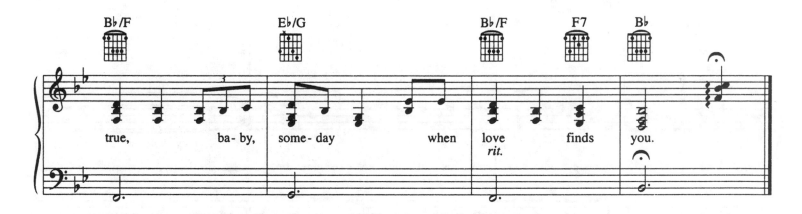

*Additional lyrics*

2. Love is the power that makes your heart beat,
   It can make you move mountains, make you drop to your knees.
   When it finally hits you, you won't know what to do,
   There's nothing you can say when love finds you.

3. *Instrumental*
   And when you least expect it, it will finally come true,
   There's nothing you can say when love finds you.

When Love Finds You - 4 - 4

# YOU WIN MY LOVE

Words and Music by
ROBERT JOHN ''MUTT'' LANGE

look-in' for a lov-er who can rev his lit-tle en - gine up.

He can have a fif-ty five Chev-y or a fan-cy lit-tle pick-up truck.

\* Vocal sung one octave lower.

You Win My Love - 6 - 1

Verses 2, 3 & 4:

2. If he's got a cool Cad-il-lac with a jac-
3.4. *See additional lyrics*

uz-zi in the back, I'm in,___ oh, yeah.___ 'Cause I'm a

class-y lit-tle chas-sis who's a-hunt-in' for a heart__ to win.__

*Bridge:*

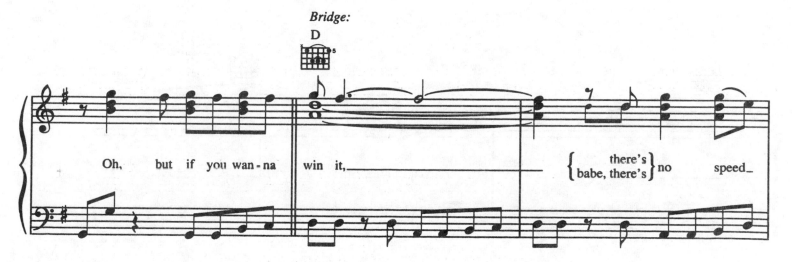

Oh, but if you wan-na win it,_____ { there's / babe, there's } no speed__

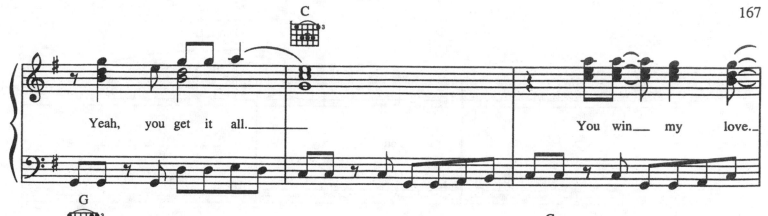

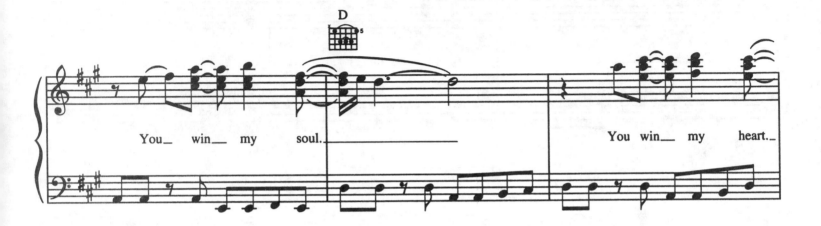

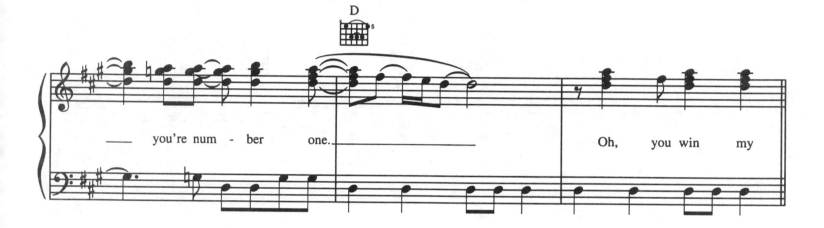

*Verse 2:*
Oh, I'm a crazy little lady,
Yeah, the kind you just can't slow down, oh no.
I need a sixty-five cylinder racy little run around town.
*(To Bridge:)*

*Verse 3:*
I want a heartbreak Harley,
A full of steam, dream machine,
Or just a little late night
Sexy, long limousine.
*(To Bridge:)*

# YOUR LOVE AMAZES ME

Words and Music by
CHUCK JONES and AMANDA HUNT

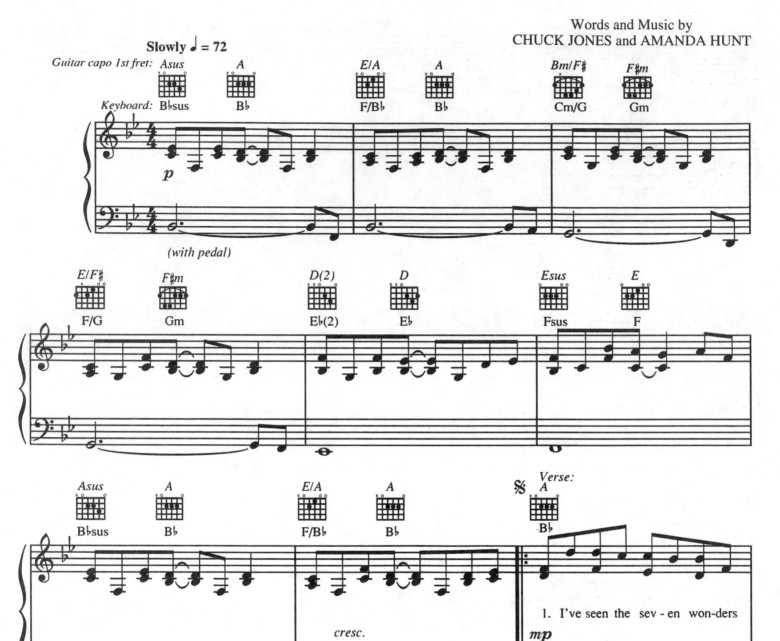

Your Love Amazes Me - 4 - 1

But they ain't noth-in', ba - by, your love a - maz - es me.

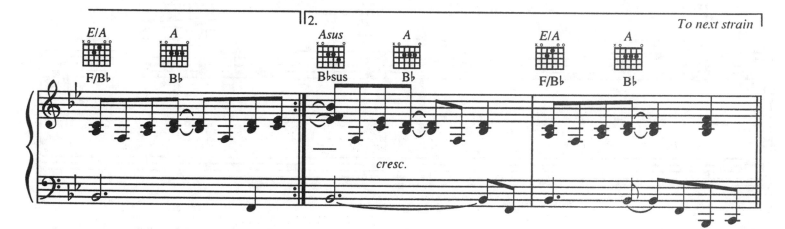

To next strain

cresc.

Chorus:

cresc.

*mf* Don't you ev - er doubt this love of mine.

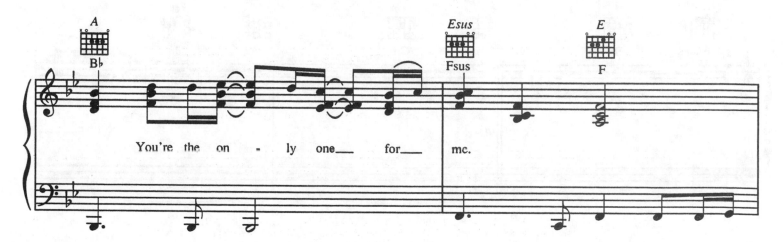

You're the on - ly one__ for__ me.

You give me hope, you give__ me rea - son.    You give me some - thing__ to be - lieve__ in.

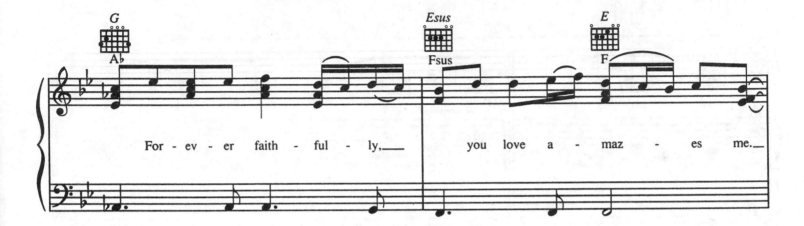

For - ev - er faith - ful - ly,__ you love a - maz - es me.__

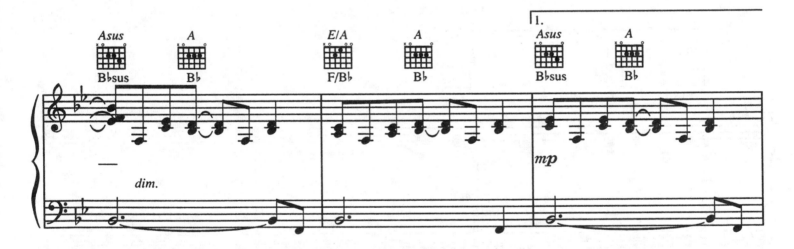

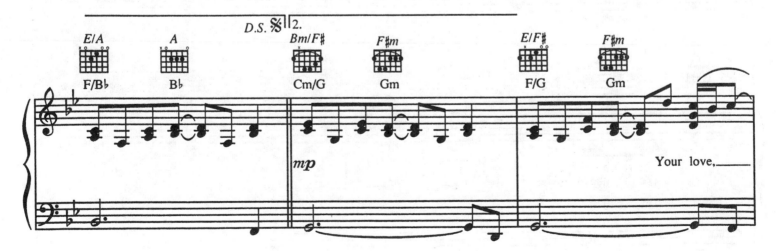

Your love,__

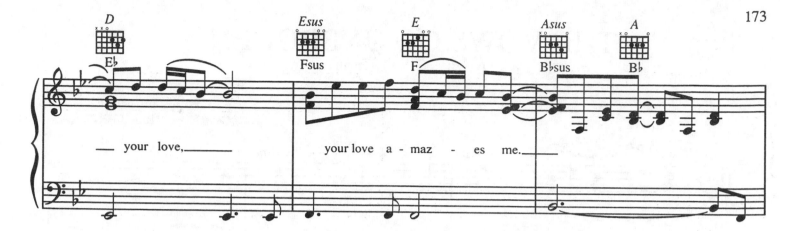

your love,_____ your love a - maz - es me._____

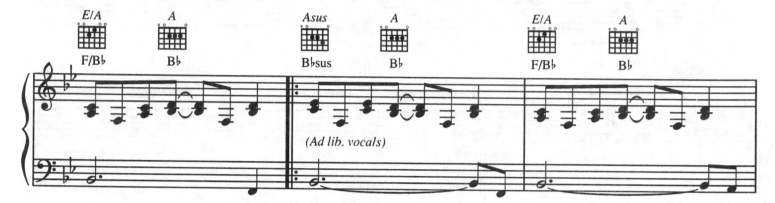

*(Ad lib. vocals)*

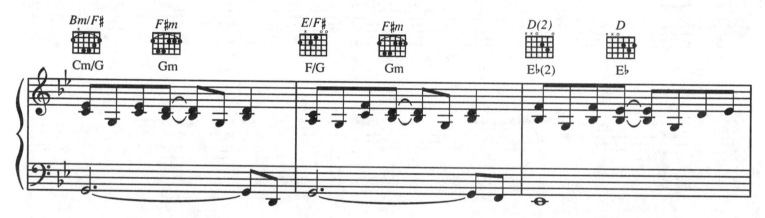

*Repeat ad lib. and fade*

*Verse 2:*
I've seen a sunset that would make you cry,
And colors of a rainbow reaching 'cross the sky.
The moon in all its phases, but
Your love amazes me.
*To Chorus:*

*Verse 3:*
I've prayed for miracles that never came.
I got down on my knees in the pouring rain.
But only you could save me,
Your love amazes me.
*(To Chorus:)*

# THE VOWS GO UNBROKEN
## (Always True to You)

Words and Music by
GARY BURR and ERIC KAZ

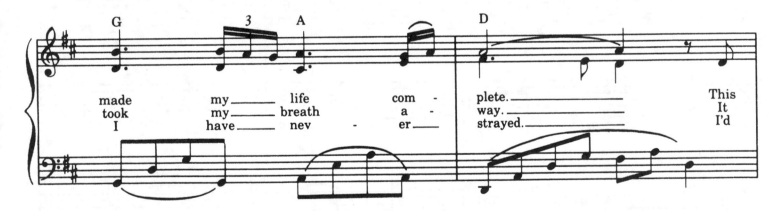

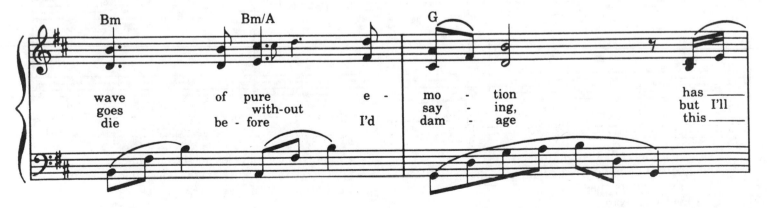

The Vows Go Unbroken - 3 - 1

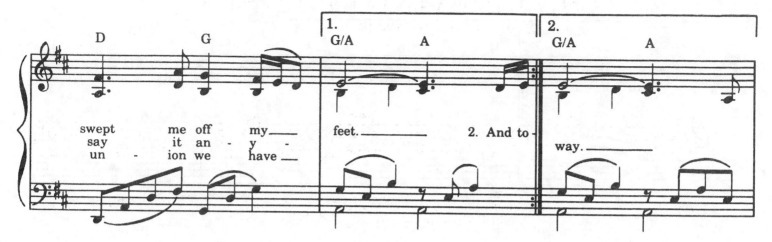

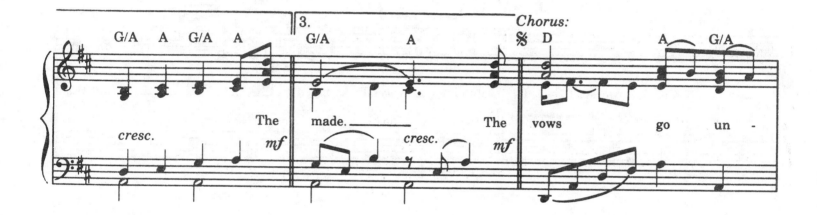

The Vows Go Unbroken - 3 - 2

From the Original Motion Picture Soundtrack "BEACHES"

# THE WIND BENEATH MY WINGS

Words and Music by
LARRY HENLEY and JEFF SILBAR

**Gently flowing, in 2**

*pedal throughout*

It must have been cold there in my shad - ow, ___

to nev - er have sun - light on your

The Wind beneath My Wings - 7 - 1

182